BRIGHT NOTES

THE MAJOR POEMS BY DYLAN THOMAS

Intelligent Education

Nashville, Tennessee

BRIGHT NOTES: The Major Poems
www.BrightNotes.com

No part of this publication may be used or reproduced in any manner whatsoever without written permission, except in the case of brief quotations in critical articles and reviews. For permissions, contact Influence Publishers http://www.influencepublishers.com.

ISBN: 978-1-645424-58-1 (Paperback)
ISBN: 978-1-645424-59-8 (eBook)

Published in accordance with the U.S. Copyright Office Orphan Works and Mass Digitization report of the register of copyrights, June 2015.

Originally published by Monarch Press.
H Richmond Neuville, 1965
2020 Edition published by Influence Publishers.

Interior design by Lapiz Digital Services. Cover Design by Thinkpen Designs.

Printed in the United States of America.

Library of Congress Cataloging-in-Publication Data forthcoming.
Names: Intelligent Education
Title: BRIGHT NOTES: The Major Poems
Subject: STU004000 STUDY AIDS / Book Notes

CONTENTS

1)	Introduction to Dylan Thomas	1
2)	18 Poems	12
3)	Twenty-Five Poems	31
4)	The Map of Love	55
5)	Deaths and Entrances	70
6)	In Country Sleep	96
7)	Miscellaneous	102
8)	Poems	107
9)	Critical Commentary	111
10)	Bibliography	117

INTRODUCTION TO DYLAN THOMAS

DYLAN THOMAS' LIFE

Youth (1914-1936). Dylan Marlais Thomas first screamed at the light of life in Swansea, Wales, on October 22, 1914, the son of a teacher of English in a grammar school. He attended the Swansea Grammar School from 1925 to 1931, which was the only formal education he had except the liberty to read whatever he wanted in his father's library. He was an editor of the *Swansea Grammar School Magazine* for his last two years of school and published in it twenty-seven poems, two short stories, two essays, and various parodies and notes. His early schoolboy poems also appeared in the *Western Mail* and the *Boys Own Paper*. After graduation he worked on the staff of the *South Wales Daily Post* for a year. During the first four years of the 1930's he continued to write verse, keeping them in notebooks which are now in the Lockwood Library of the University of Buffalo. Dylan Thomas gave up hack journalism in January, 1933, and in February won the BBC (British Broadcasting Corporation) Competition with "The Romantic Isle," a poem which is no longer extant. May 18th saw the first London publication of one of his poems, "And death shall have no dominion," in the *New English Weekly*. He also published verse between 1933 and 1934 in *Adelphi, Sunday Referee, Listener*, and *New Verse*. In November, 1934, he moved to London to learn the poet's craft, beginning his "bohemian" life against the tyranny of respectability and propriety.

On December 18, 1934, when Thomas was twenty years old, *18 Poems* was published in London by the *Sunday Referee* and the Parton Bookshop, where it caused a great deal of excitement because of its obscurity and violent **imagery**. Included in this volume were "I See the Boys of Summer," "If I Were Tickled By the Rub of Love," "Especially When the October Wind." These eighteen poems concern personal problems - sexual and poetic creation - and the ubiquitous cycle of birth, death, and rebirth. Between December of 1935 and the following February, Thomas was back in Swansea, preparing the manuscript for his *Twenty-five Poems*, which was published in London by J. M. Dent and Son on September 10, 1936. This volume brought him more fame and enthusiastic praise from Edith Sitwell. Among the poems published in this volume were "Should Lanterns Shine," "And Death Shall Have No Dominion," and the "Altar-wise By Owl-Light" sonnets. In these two volumes a multiplicity of ideas and emotions are put forth with a small vocabulary. Obscurity results, however, because words are repeated in a variety of nuances of sense and meaning, and because of the originality of his **imagery** and technique. From this period Thomas began to approach a religious feeling which would become more dominant in his later poetry.

Middle Period And War Years (1937-1946). Dylan Thomas married the beautiful Caitlin Macnamara in July, 1937, living mainly at Ringwood, Hants, until April, 1938. By July they settled in Laugharne, a small fishing village in South Wales. During this period Thomas was revising his early poetry and publishing verse and stories in several magazines. His first son, Llewelyn, was born in January, 1939, and Dylan's **themes** expanded to reflect a feeling for others, the threat of war, and his family. On

August 24, J. M. Dent and Son published his *The Map of Love*, containing sixteen poems and several stories. The stories are semi-surrealistic, his prose fleurs du mal, of little artistic value, but he subsequently abandoned the symbolic prose of his early stories and began to write stories of human beings living as he remembered as a child. Afterward, Thomas collected several stories and published them on April 4, 1940, in the comic *Portrait of the Artist as a Young Dog*. During the war years he resided mostly in Wales, coming to London occasionally, writing poetry, short fiction and film scripts, and performing on the BBC as either an actor or a reader. On February 27, 1946 *Deaths and Entrances* was published by Dent. This edition contained twenty-four poems, mostly from 1939-1945, but included revisions of "The Hunchback in the Park" and "On the Marriage of a Virgin," written in 1932 and 1933, respectively. In these later poems the symbolism has given place to **metaphor**. Much of his poetry became more straightforward and clear, his movement toward the light was accompanied by a simplification in style and loss of obscurity (for the most part). His **themes** expanded to include religious statements, childhood innocence, and a mature human awareness of experience.

Maturity (1947-1953). Thomas remained in London after the war, continuing his BBC Home Broadcasts, several of which were published in *Quite Early One Morning* (1955). During the summer of 1947 the Thomases went to Italy, returning to South Leigh, Oxford, in September. During this period Thomas wrote the film script, *The Beach at Falesa*. In April, 1949, they returned to Laugharne. Because of financial need, Dylan Thomas visited the United States three times on reading tours during the early 1950's. Here he discovered Third Avenue and drank whiskey instead of his customary beer. After he returned from his first trip in May, 1951, he wrote "In the White Giant's Thigh," "Poem On His Birthday," "Do Not Go Gentle Into That Good Night," and

"Lament," which were published on February 28, 1952 in the book, *In Country Sleep*. In 1952 he wrote the "Author's Prologue" to his preparation of the *Collected Poems*, which included all the poems that he wished to leave to the world. The *Collected Poems* was published by Dent on November 10, 1952, in the new order that Thomas had arranged and with his "Note" stating that the poems were written for the love of man and in praise of God. He returned to the United States in the spring of 1953 for the first performance of *Under Milk Wood* and again in the fall of the year. Thomas died suddenly in New York on November 9, 1953, from an attack of the delirium tremens brought on by his excessive drinking and bohemian way of life.

TWENTIETH-CENTURY POETRY

The Georgians (ca. 1912-1920's) were a group of poets including John Drinkwater (1882-1937) and Rupert Brooke (1887-1915), who reacted against the affectations of late-Victorian poetry and attempted to make it more masculine. They followed A. E. Houseman's bucolic return to nature and uncritically followed the spirit of Wordsworth's lyrics. They echoed Wordsworth's assurance in natural beauty and extended his confidence in the benign power of the country, ignoring and avoiding its uglier implications.

The War Poets, especially Siegfried Sassoon (1886-1967) and Wilfred Owen (1893-1918), a Welshman, were originally in the Georgian camp but later were influenced by the harsh realities of the Great War. Their poetry was pungent and biting, and Owens was fond of **assonance** and versatile in rhythm.

The Imagists (1915-1920's) were contemporaneous with the Georgian movement, but they were primarily experimentalists. They were influenced by the critic, T. E. Hulme, who tried to apply to poetry Henri Bergson's concept of time as a flow in the mind. An imagist poem was, therefore, an attempt to express the flow of experience in concrete terms. The imagists did away with decorative statements and used the language of common speech. They desired to present an "image" which evoked sensations that had a foundation in experience. Some important poets of this movement were Amy Lowell (1874-1925), Richard Aldington (1892-1962), Ezra Pound (1885-1972), and Hilda Doolittle, "H. D." (1886-1961).

T. S. Eliot (1888-1964) tried to fuse feeling and thought in his poetry. As a young man he put himself under the influence of the French Symbolists (late 19th century) and the English **Metaphysical** poets, correctly perceiving that the **Metaphysical** poets merged thought and feeling but not realizing that the French Symbolists abhorred the intellect in poetry and stressed feeling and sensuality. The younger poets of the day admired and imitated, not Eliot's content and philosophy, but his technique. "The Love Song of J. Alfred Prufrock" (1917) was a description of outward scenes which serve as symbols to illustrate the vacuity and frustration of our moribund civilization. "The Waste Land" (1922) was a diagnosis of the ills of society and a realization of the need for regeneration.

W. H. Auden (1907-1973) began publishing poetry characterized by disgust, cynicism and radicalism in the late 1920's and 1930's, in which he diagnosed modern life in terms of Freud and Marx. After World War II his poetry became more exuberant and contained, at times, religious hope, that is, he had a more religious view of personal responsibility and traditional values. Auden took his poetic "wit" and **irony** from Eliot, and his metrical and verbal techniques he learned from Hopkins and Owen. He was continually experimenting in combinations of a colloquial tone and technical formality, alternating the serious and the flippant.

DYLAN THOMAS' STYLE

Language. Dylan Thomas' poetic language is rich and resonant, powerfully compelling and convincing the reader by its sound before he can comprehend its meaning. He achieves this effect by the verbal play of alliteration, **assonance**, **consonance**, and the emphatic vocabulary of active, ordinary words. Thomas loved the sound of words, perhaps too greatly, and he continuously re-used words, but in new contexts and with new connotations. He would use ordinary words, expressions and phrases, change them subtly, and present a fresh, strong image requiring, however, careful analysis in order to realize its derivation and purpose. Professor Clark Emery (*The World of Dylan Thomas*) has examined Dylan Thomas' language and found that Thomas has a working-vocabulary of about 3,600 words, most of them monosyllabic or short, relating to sense experience, and concerning the "areas of normal experience."

Meter. Thomas' meter is generally based on the number of stresses in a line rather than a sequence of stresses and slacks, although traditional meter can be found in Thomas. In the late Victorian period Gerard Manley Hopkins revived the use of "sprung rhythm" in poetry because he felt that the reader would receive more of the emotional charge of the poem by counting only the stresses instead of scanning a line according to stress and slack combinations.

INFLUENCES ON DYLAN THOMAS

Almost every critic has proclaimed at least one source for Dylan Thomas' poetry, others naming so many that Thomas' scholarship would have required more time than his creating poetry. The *18 Poems* volume was acclaimed because it was something new, original, and full of life. Any alleged source for Thomas' poetry is never a satisfactory answer for the pedant's researches in the dry-as-dust graves of libraries. The closest one can come to tracing influences on Dylan Thomas is to observe certain superficial parallels which his poetry has (whether consciously or unconsciously) with other writings. Thomas did not, of course, write in a vacuum. He certainly knew what had been done before him, but he was the continuator of a progress and not a rehasher of poetic predecessors.

Gerard Manley Hopkins is often proclaimed as Thomas' instructor in the techniques of Welsh poetry. Hopkins was interested in Welsh poetry and copied its techniques; he was interested in the flexibility of sprung rhythm and the general rising and falling movement it gave to a line; he saw natural beauty as a reflection of God; he used familiar words in startling contexts and combinations; and Hopkins was concerned with the **theme** of birth-death. All of these characteristics are also found in Thomas, but it is not likely that they derived from a close study of Hopkins. It is more probable that Thomas observed them in Hopkins and worked out the principles by himself.

James Joyce's "influence" can be chiefly observed in Thomas' short stories and in his obsession with portraits of the artist. Joyce's verbal play and insight into a cyclic process in life was probably obtained by reading a few pages of "Work in Progress" as it appeared in transition (sic) magazine.

Freud. The average student of literature is apt to lump all sexual **imagery** under the catch-phrase "Freudian." Freud's interpretation of the sexual nature of dreams, however, is a realization of the suppressed desires of the conscious being worked out in the subconscious. The poet, on the other hand, is concerned with actively and consciously collecting, evaluating and creating images in a way that goes beyond the Freudian boundaries. A poem is a conscious and deliberate arrangement of words, and any "Freudian" elements in it are elements that have transcended Freud's narrow preoccupations. Sexual symbolism and **imagery** were known and deliberately used as such thousands of years before Freud investigated sexual repressions. In addition, we have Thomas' own statement in "Replies to an Enquiry" that he went beyond Freud's limited hypothesis to achieve something deliberately poetic, howbeit sexual. But we are grateful to Freud for labelling what has been known and done since a thousand years before the Christian era.

DYLAN THOMAS AS A RELIGIOUS POET

In his "Note" to the *Collected Poems* Thomas wrote that his poems were written for the love of Man and in praise of God; he did not wish to be classified with the Biblical fool who says in his heart that there is no God. His vocation as a poet-creator was further identified as a concern for man and God in his poetry - a "justification of the ways of God to man," in the Miltonic phrase. Yet his life and legend, his conversations and bohemian poses have made it difficult to consider Thomas as a religious poet.

Thomas' father was an agnostic, and Thomas' own Christianity, after compulsory Presbyterian Sunday School and chapel as a child, was neither orthodox nor reverent. Thomas broke away from organized Christianity, but his poetry progressed increasingly toward a personal treatment and concern for God in relation to Man. Thomas reacted against the **conventions** of Welsh bourgeois morality, yet for all the sexuality in his poems he remained basically puritan.

It is through his function, or "vocation," as poet that Thomas can be considered a religious poet. "Should Lanterns Shine" (1932, rev. 1935) is an illustration of the emptiness and uselessness of a religious belief which can not withstand the light of reason. "I Have Longed to Move Away" (1933, rev. 1935) declares that Thomas desires to renounce the empty and ritualistic Christian religion, but he is afraid; yet, he does not wish to die hypocritically following a convention.

"This Bread I Break" (1933, rev. 1936) indicates that sacramental bread and wine were once part of nature. The flesh and blood of the Christ which are symbolized in the eucharist were once living members of nature. By destroying them, man participates in the sacramental communion of God, man and nature. In "Incarnate Devil" (1933, rev. 1936) Thomas attacks a weak and ineffectual God who has condemned sex as devilish and praised abstinence as divine. The "Altarwise By Owl-light" **sonnets** (1935) illustrate a movement from religious confusion to religious prophecy and apocalypse.

"The Spire Cranes" (1931, rev. 1937) attacks the dogmatism of organized religion which imprisons the free spirit, but the sound of church bells is able to escape the restraint of the steeple. "There Was a Saviour" (1940) is an attack on those who follow the form and letter of Christianity without following the spirit. The "**Ballad** of the Long-legged Bait" (1941) depicts the **epic** vanquishment of sinful lust by man's own powers to sublimate his lust to a higher love. "Vision and Prayer" (1944) is a record of Thomas' movement from lost darkness to found light, culminating in a prayer that he be absorbed into the wound of the Crucifixion. In "The Conversation of Prayer" (1945) the sincere, conversational type of prayer is granted but the ritualistic formula is not.

"In Country Sleep" (1947) proclaims that faith in a holy Nature will conquer the fears of childhood's fantasies and of Death. "Over Sir John's hill" (1948) praises the life and death process of Nature. "Poem On His Birthday" (1950) indicates that Thomas is arriving at a triumphant faith in the holiness of Nature and natural process. In the "Author's Prologue" (1952) the poet, because of his love for man and God, desires to save all Nature from the flood of fear and rage by constructing poetical arks of love.

Dylan Thomas was not a holy priest or a saint but an earthy man in love with life and nature. He saw beyond the physical limits of existence to a personal relationship of poet and man with a Divine Creator. As a poet, Thomas was also a creator, and so he shared with God something beyond the domain of ordinary men. Through his poetry he sought to juxtapose the mysteries of God and nature in order to clarify man's place in the universal scheme. It was this attempt to justify God's ways that became Thomas' dominant thematic concern.

PROGRESSION OF THEMES

"Where Once the Twilight Locks No Longer" (1933) traces the progress of poetic creativity from the poem's inception, to the presentation of the completed poem after the creative imagination had been drained. This poem, furthermore, contains a statement of Thomas' **themes** (the unity of womb and tomb) and a recapitulation in which the poet declares that he must free himself from the drugged dream. "Especially When the October Wind" (1934) concerns the making of poetry and Thomas' desire to replace his weak habits of writing with more vital and forceful ones. He is afraid that he is losing his poetical powers. "To-day, This Insect" (1930, rev. 1936) is a statement presented on intricate parallel levels of the creation and process toward death of the universe, the child, and Thomas' poetry, concluding with an affirmation that his poetic subject will be man.

"Foster the Light" (1934, rev. 1936) is an exhortation to master all the forces of life and nature and to produce the shapes of poetry. "When All My Five and Country Senses See" (1933, rev. 1938) is a manifesto of poetic intent, **theme** and method, that all his senses will function together to experience and write about life. "Once It Was the Colour Of Saying" (1933, rev. 1938) indicates the necessity of revising his approach to poetry, to cast off the writing of memories of childhood. "On No Work Of Words" (1933, rev. 1938) recounts a period of aridity during which Thomas refuses to abandon his poetic integrity and copy his own and others' poetic themes. "Love In the Asylum" (ca. 1941) depicts the return of poetic inspiration in the form of a mad girl. "In My Craft Or Sullen Art" (1945) is a poetic manifesto that Thomas' craft is exercised only for lovers, who, however, pay it no heed.

MAJOR POEMS

18 POEMS

I SEE THE BOYS OF SUMMER

Introduction. This poem from *18 Poems* was first composed in April, 1934 and published in the June issue of *New Verse*. "I See The Boys of Summer" is in the form of a three-part dialogue between the speaker and the boys of summer.

SUMMARY

The speaker observes and comments on the foolishness and sterility of the boys' masturbating. They deny, or kill, the process of gestation and birth. The boys in turn justify themselves, replying that sexual union produces death not life, that creation is but a prelude to destruction. The third part is like a palinode, alternating lines of dialogue, restating the previously developed themes.

Analysis. In the first part the speaker contrasts summer as a season and as a representation of youth and lust with the winter of onanism which freezes the soil (prevents the harvest of birth) and love. From these boys nothing shall come. The boys reply that they deny the normal sexual process in order to challenge time - the cycle of gestation and birth leads only to death. In the final **stanza** of part two the boys join Christmas and the Crucifixion together, another instance of life leading to death. But the implication of rebirth is introduced; there is still promise in the boys. The third part is a summary dialogue, consolidating the previous statements, and indicating that the debate ends without a definite resolution.

Form And Style. The poem is written in six-line **stanzas** which imperfectly **rhyme** aabcbc. Each part ends with the same first three words. The meter is iambic **pentameter** except for the second line of each stanza which is **trimeter** and has one iamb composed of three short syllables. **Alliteration** and **assonance** are prominent. Adolescent phallic symbolism is observable throughout.

WHEN ONCE THE TWILIGHT LOCKS NO LONGER

Introduction. "When Once the Twilight Locks No Longer" was composed on November 11, 1933, and published for the first time in June, 1934 issue of *New Verse*. It was included in *18 Poems*.

SUMMARY

This poem considers the process of creation and destruction on three levels: sexual creation, the Divine Creation, and poetic creation.

Analysis. The first **stanza** indicates the time when, sexually, the penis opened its "twilight locks" and the womb took in the semen from the genitals. In the scheme of the Divine Creation it refers to the first days of Genesis when the universe "was without form, and void," and God said "Let the waters under the heaven be gathered together unto one place, and let the dry land appear." Poetically the **stanza** refers to the beginning of poetic activity.

The second **stanza** relates the bringing of the baby to light from the womb, the sending of man (the Adam myth) into the world, and the presentation of the completed poem after the creative imagination had been drained. The third **stanza** focuses on the created object, the child who has a dream and drowns his father's magic, man who, through Adam, rejects the Divine system, or the poetic words of the imagination.

The fourth and fifth **stanzas** describe this dream. The child now has his own sexual experiences, prolonging the process of creation - destruction, womb-tomb. On the divine level the dream indicates man's rejection of God for the delusions of the world. The **stanzas** further indicate the **theme** of the creator's poems, that of the unity of womb and tomb.

If the poem is read either sexually or as referring to the creative imagination, then the sixth **stanza** is a recapitulation. If the poem is read as a history of Divine Creation, then this **stanza** is a reference to the Incarnation and Crucifixion of Christ. The final **stanza** is an exhortation to the active life; the creature must awake and work in the world, abandon the thankless drugged dream and free himself.

Form And Style. "When Once The Twilight Locks No Longer" contains seven stanzas, having near **rhymes** which exhibit **consonance**: aabccb.

A PROCESS IN THE WEATHER OF THE HEART

Introduction. This short poem was composed February 2, 1934, and first appeared in the *Sunday Referee* of February 11, 1934, before it was published in *18 Poems*.

SUMMARY

> The natural process of life, seen in various aspects, is really only a process to death.

Analysis. Thomas contrasts a series of disparate images of the external world and the body (internal world) of man to demonstrate that the goal of life is death and decay. The life-creating of the sex act symbolizes the beginning of another process of death. There is no difference between the living and the dead, both are ghosts.

Form And Style. This poem is composed of five stanzas, the first, third and fifth having sixth lines, the second and fourth three lines. The larger **stanzas rhyme** aabccb, the shorter stanzas rhyme approximately cba. There are semi-colons which retard the sentences in every second and fifth line, except for the last fifth line. The meter is iambic pentameter.

BEFORE I KNOCKED

Introduction. "Before I Knocked" was composed on September 6, 1933, and first published in *18 Poems*.

SUMMARY

> This poem appears to be a monologue of a sperm cell before it is ejaculated into the womb, a sperm cell that foreknows its future life, suffering, and death.

Analysis. This remarkable sperm cell has a prescience about its future suffering and death, and seems to refer to that particular sperm cell which would develop into Christ. But it is also possible to interpret the poem as relating to every man who, by being a man, vaguely is similar to Christ. Therefore every sperm cell has some participation in God's nature and is, in a certain sense, divine.

Form And Style. In a bold attempt to understand God-as-Man, Thomas treats Man-as-God. This daring and confusing **metaphor** is continued throughout the entire eight **stanzas** and gives the poem a powerful force. The first seven **stanzas** are composed of six lines and the last of four lines. The **rhyme** scheme is near-rhyme, exhibiting **consonance**, ababab.

THE FORCE THAT THROUGH THE GREEN FUSE DRIVES THE FLOWER

Introduction. This poem, among Thomas' best, was composed on October 12, 1933, when Thomas was not quite nineteen years old, and published in the *Sunday Referee* of October 29, 1933. It also appeared in *18 Poems*.

SUMMARY

> The same force that drives the external world of nature also drives the internal world of the poet's body in the same process of life and death.

Analysis. Through a series of counter-statements Thomas sketches the parallels of nature and man. The same force that gives life to plants also gives life to the poet, and is similarly their mutual destroyer. The same force that moves water similarly moves the poet's blood, and just as similarly removes this vital element. The same hand that whirls pool waters hauls on a shroud and hangs a man. The time that sustains life also takes away life, and the loss of blood at death eases the pains of death. To all these antitheses the poet is unable to explain to the particular aspect of nature or his body "how" they occur.

Form And Style. The poem is composed of five five-line **stanzas** and a concluding **couplet**. Every fourth line begins with the same word, and every fifth line (except in the first **stanza**) with the same word. Each five-line **stanza** is composed of three lines which state the antitheses, and two lines which express the poet's inability to explain them. The **rhyme** is approximate, ababa, with the fourth **stanza** rhyming aabab. Thomas uses sprung rhythm to give a rising and falling movement to each **stanza**. The poem is tied together by the repetition of the same initial words, by semi-colons in the second lines of each **stanza**, by **imagery** based on the elements and the parts of the body, and by the repetition of similar words from one **stanza** to the next.

MY HERO BARES HIS NERVES

Introduction. This poem was composed on September 17, 1933, and first published in *18 Poems*.

SUMMARY

My "Hero" is a description on one level of the act of masturbation and, on the other level, of the process of writing.

Analysis. The "Hero" is the speaker's hand performing the act of masturbation and frustrating the act of love. The hero is also the hand that writes a poem. The creative mind of the poet stimulates the brain, the spine, the nerves, and eventually the hand of the poet to put on paper his standard **theme** of birth and death. The poet's last line indicates that he pulls the chain on the toilet and flushes it, causing the cistern to move. The image is immediately relatable to masturbation; its poetic implication may be that the act of writing is a purging or catharsis of the emotions.

Form And Style. The poem **rhymes** in the standard near-rhyme of consonant sounds, ababa. The structure consists of four five-line stanzas. The rhythm is constructed of alternating five-stress and three-stress lines.

WHERE ONCE THE WATERS OF YOUR FACE

Introduction. "Where Once the Waters Of Your Face" was composed on March 18, 1934. It appeared in the *Sunday Referee* on March 25, before it was published in *18 Poems*.

SUMMARY

> This poem relates the cyclic process of birth, death, and rebirth.

Analysis. The speaker likens his girl to the sea and tells her that, where once her waters moved to his or mermen's sexual intercourse with her, all is now dry; where once she was fruitful, now she is sterile. But although her lovebeds are dry, coral beds are being constructed now that will last until faith dies. Although her womb is sterile, it will once again be fertile.

Form And Style. This short, twenty-four-line poem is divided into four stanzas. The **rhyme** scheme, as is expected now, is near or approximate, abcabc. There are three stresses in each line. Lines one, two, four and five have eight syllables, lines three and six have six syllables.

IF I WERE TICKLED BY THE RUB OF LOVE

Introduction. This poem was written on April 30, 1934 and was first published in *New Verse* in August of that same year before appearing in *18 Poems*.

SUMMARY

> If the speaker were stimulated and amused by sexual intercourse he would not fear the intimations of death. He questions what is this "rub" and concludes that his **metaphor** will be Man.

Analysis. The first four **stanzas** repeat parallel conditions that if the speaker were tickled by the rub of love he would not fear the sin of the apple in Eden or punishment for sin by flood, he would not fear death by law or by war or by the cruciform sign of crusaders, and he would not fear the propagation of death through sex. The last three **stanzas** begin with the statement that the world is half the devil's and half the speaker's, who watches the phallic worm of death in his hand wearing life away. The only rub that tickles is the act of masturbation, but it can never produce a laugh. The final **stanza** asks what is the rub, what is to be the subject-matter of his poetry. Is it to be sex, death in the womb, or religion? The speaker rejects these possibilities and concludes that Man will be his metaphor.

Form And Style. "If I Were Tickled" is composed of seven **stanzas** of seven lines each, having occasional near-rhyme based on consonants, but in no sustained pattern. Structural unity is achieved by parallelism and rhetorical repetition.

OUR EUNUCH DREAMS

Introduction. "Our Eunuch Dreams" was composed in March, 1934, and first published in the April issue of *New Verse*. It appears in *18 Poems*.

SUMMARY

> Thomas compares the impotence and unreality of life to the unreality of the movies. Modern life is a false and empty dream which man must reject and destroy in order to bring about a "real" future life.

Analysis. In the first part the sexual dreams of an impotent eunuch are equated with unreal modern life. In the second part love is shown to be false in the modern world since our standards are based on the lies of the movie screen. The third part asks which of these aspects is the world, both are sleeping and not reality. The fourth part identifies the world as a dream in which what is unreal is real, and contains an exhortation to destroy this dream-fantasy so that men will be fit for real life.

Form And Style. There is near-rhyme of consonants in these four curtal **sonnets** of ten lines. The **rhyme** scheme is abcabc dede. The sestet of the **sonnet** contains four-stress lines (1 and 2, 4 and 5) and three-stress lines (lines 3 and 6). The quatrain contains four-stress lines. Caesura occurs in all the four-stress lines.

ESPECIALLY WHEN THE OCTOBER WIND

Introduction. Composed in 1934, this poem was first published in the *Listener* of October 24, 1934 and then in *18 Poems*.

SUMMARY

"Especially When the October Wind" treats the making of poetry and Thomas' desire to remove his weak and shadowy habits of writing and use vital and effective poetic statements. He is afraid that he is losing his power.

Analysis. On a cold, windy October (his birth month) the poet is walking by the seaside, casting shadows (his old poems) on the sand. Passionately, he determines to shed his previous technique (which was as vital as shadows and crabs) and drain his words. He desires to leave his tower of words and participate in life, treating women and children in strong **metaphors** of trees. The mechanical clock indicates that time is passing quickly and winter is approaching; he must hurry to write in the symbols of the signal grass or tell of the raven's sins. Especially when the cold October wind of the lack of poetic inspiration comes, Thomas concludes, the poet desires to make poetry of heartless words, but his heart is drained.

Form And Style. Written in anapests the four **stanzas** have a rhyme scheme of abbacddc. **Alliteration** and **assonance** abound in the lines.

WHEN, LIKE A RUNNING GRAVE

Introduction. Composed sometime after April, 1934, this poem did not appear in print until it was published in *18 Poems*.

SUMMARY

Thomas' poem is a plea for deliverance from sexual desires, for love is death.

Analysis. When time tracks you down like a hunter, love is like a turtle in a hearse (womb). Age comes like a tailor with a pair of scissors to fit him for time's jacket, and only the abstinence from sexual intercourse will deliver him from the straight grave. The male organ, that cross of fever, is only Cadaver's shoot which propagates doom. Love is a trick, life is not continued by sexual intercourse but another death is brought into the world.

Form And Style. "When, Like a Running Grave" is composed of ten stanzas of five lines each. The first four lines are of ten syllables, the fifth line is short, generally of four syllables. The near-rhyme of **assonance** is in an abcba scheme. The long lines contain four stresses, the short lines contain two stresses.

FROM LOVE'S FIRST FEVER TO HER PLAGUE

Introduction. This poem was written on October 14, 1933, and published in *Criterion* of October, 1934. It was next published in *18 Poems*.

SUMMARY

> The poem depicts the growth of the man from embryo to adolescent poet, progressing from the many concretes to the one universal theme.

Analysis. From the fire and pleasures of intercourse and his conception to his birth, the world to Thomas was one windy nothing and the earth and sky were as two mountains meeting. The boy grew and progressed, first distinguishing the many concretes in the world, then uniting them through speech. As a poet he is inspired by the code of night (the **theme** of womb-tomb, creation-destruction) and expresses this single idea in many-sounding poetry.

Form And Style. The poem is irregular, the first and third stanzas having nine lines, the second and fourth having six lines, but the fifth **stanza** contains eight lines and the sixth stanza three lines. The final **stanza** returns to nine lines. It is

blank verse, without **rhyme**, and the length of the lines varies considerably from long to short.

IN THE BEGINNING

Introduction. "In The Beginning" was composed on September 18, 1933, and was not published until its inclusion in *18 Poems*. It was revised from its earlier form in April, 1934.

SUMMARY

> This poem is an account of the creation of the universe with parallel implications of poetic and sexual creation.

Analysis. Thomas uses the Gospel of John to underline the work of Genesis in illuminating the Creation of the World and the Word. This poem is one of Thomas' most difficult to understand and there are as many interpretations as there are critics. The mysteries of eternity, the Trinity, and the Incarnation are mingled with the act of creation. As a poem describing the act of poetic creation, "In The Beginning" chronicles the progress of fiery inspiration to the word to the organization of the word. And simultaneously, sexual interpretations can be found in the ambiguous phraseology.

Form And Style. There is occasional near-rhyme in several of the lines but it is not characteristic of the poem as an entity. There are five **stanzas** of six lines each. There are four stresses in each line.

LIGHT BREAKS WHERE NO SUN SHINES

Introduction. This poem was composed on November 20, 1933, and published in the *Listener* of March 14, 1934. It was among the poems included in *18 Poems*.

SUMMARY

> This poem is a parallel development of the body of man toward death and the simultaneous development of the decaying corpse to fertilize the soil and produce new life.

Analysis. The poem is built up on a series of **metaphysical** conceits which are contradictory. The first half of each **stanza** deals with a period in a man's life, the second half with a period in the process of a corpse's decomposition. Thus, **stanza** one presents the reader with copulation and conception (life) and initial stages of decay (death). The second stanza recounts the first sexual urgings of adolescence, the second part treats the assimilation of the corpse's life-forces with the stars. **Stanza** three depicts the maturity of adult life and the return of the life-forces in the form of rain. The fourth **stanza** contrasts old age in a man with the old age of winter presaging springtime. The final **stanza** presents a reversal of the images; the man has died and been laid in the grave, the life-forces of the corpse are producing fresh life in the soil.

Form And Style. The rhyme-scheme is based on consonants (near-rhyme) in an abccba form. Every third and fifth line is a short line in these six-line stanzas, with the familiar four-stress and two-stress pattern.

BRIGHT NOTES STUDY GUIDE

I FELLOWED SLEEP

Introduction. "I Fellowed Sleep" was composed on October 5, 1993, and not published until it appeared in *18 Poems*.

SUMMARY

> The poem seems to be Thomas the son's appreciations of his father's religious views and Thomas the poet's resolution to follow his father's aspirations in his poetry.

Analysis. Thomas falls asleep and dreams that he flees the earth and ascends naked to a point above the stars. There he weeps with his mother's ancestors. He extols his father, and the ghost, perhaps his mother instead of her ancestors, realistically replies that after all his father is a mortal. The ghost fades and the matter of the living air raises up its voice. Thomas describes his vision, contrasting the light sleeping on the stars and the deep waking on the world. The final **stanza** declares that there is a ladder to the sun which his father, an old man, is climbing in his ghostly form in the rain. The spirit of man, although mad, must still climb forward to the sun, and not remain earth-bound.

Form And Style. The rhythm of this poem is achieved by four-stress lines with a caesura separating the stresses into groups of two. The rhyme-scheme is in a repeated pattern of abaab cdcdc efeef, etc., based on the ubiquitous near-rhyme which Thomas employs. This near-rhyme is both consonantal and assonantal.

I DREAMED MY GENESIS

Introduction. This poem was composed sometime between April, 1934 and the appearance of *18 Poems* on December 18, 1934, in which volume it appeared.

SUMMARY

Thomas' intimations of mortality are the **theme** again in this life-death, womb-tomb poem, conception and birth being graphically described in terms of sexual intercourse.

Analysis. Thomas' sexual symbols are so obvious and universal that detailed analysis is unnecessary. The worm is a symbol for the penis and also a symbol for the destructiveness of death. Its violence is reflected in the violent entry of copulation which is extended to an equation of the beginnings of life (conception) with the beginnings of the process which leads to death.

Form And Style. The **rhyme** is based on the terminal sound of the words. Thus the near-rhyme of consonants is aaab in the first four stanzas, aaba in the fifth **stanza**, aaab in the sixth stanza, and aaaa in the final stanza. The first three lines of each **stanza** contain a pause before the final word, and the final word is grammatically joined with the following line, thus creating a strong effect and concentration of emotion on the terminal words.

BRIGHT NOTES STUDY GUIDE

MY WORLD IS PYRAMID

Introduction. "My World is Pyramid" was composed between April and December, 1934. It appeared first in the December, 1934, issue of *New Verse* before its publication in *18 Poems*.

SUMMARY

> The first part of this womb-tomb poem is a rhetorical discussion of the divided nature of an, as yet, unconceived embryo, and in the second part this embryo resolves the problem of death-life in his womb world.

Analysis. It is not until the last **stanza** of the second part that we learn the identity of the speaker. The first part indicates that this unconceived child is composed of two halves, one half deriving from the corrosive and poisoning sperm of his father, the other half from the milky secretions of the mother's lubricating glands when sexual intercourse unites the halves in a crippling womb. The second part continues the unconceived embryo's meditation on his world, expressed in terms of war, battle and death. The conclusion is that the activity of the genitalia produces only death.

Form And Style. The near-rhyme is developed in an ababcc pattern. As in almost all Thomas' poems, **alliteration** and **assonance** are ever-present, and the rhythm is achieved by four-stress lines in each six-line **stanza**, with the final line a short two-stress line. Each part contains five stanzas.

ALL ALL AND ALL THE DRY WORLD'S LEVER

Introduction. This poem was also composed in the year 1934 and did not appear in print until its publication in *18 Poems*.

SUMMARY

> The sterile, mechanical world, which has been made impotent by government and business, is defeated and rejuvenated by sexual copulation.

Analysis. The first part of this tripartite poem indicates that the world is dry because of industrial destruction and governmental regulations, and asks the poet's genitals how they will be the lever of this dry world. The second part tells his flesh and organ not to fear this industrial world. The final part proclaims that sexual activity and coupling will produce fertility in the dry world and all will flower again.

Form And Style. Each of the three parts is composed of two stanzas (near) rhyming abacbc dedfef. The rhythm is sprung, having four stresses to a line. There is very little **alliteration** but **assonance** is found throughout.

QUESTIONS ON 18 POEMS

Question. What are the major **themes** of *18 Poems*?

Answer. The major **theme** is an awareness of the destructive process of time in its cycle of birth, death and rebirth, coupled with a thematic fear that sexual intercourse does not create life but continues the process of death. Poetic creation is also an important concern.

Question. Is it possible to make a general assessment of Thomas' style in these eighteen poems?

Answer. Yes. Generally these poems are tightly structured and intricately unified. The poems are rich in **imagery** and symbolism, but the monotonous presentation of movement and rhythm detracts from any good qualities the poems might have. The continuous pounding of sterility and frustration in obscure language is over-done, and makes the reader wonder if the effort at understanding the poetry is worth it.

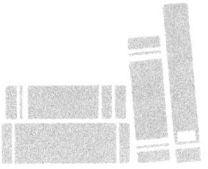

MAJOR POEMS

TWENTY-FIVE POEMS

I, IN MY INTRICATE IMAGE

Introduction. "I, in My Intricate Image" was composed about 1935, being published in *New Verse* of August-September 1935 before appearing in *Twenty-five Poems*.

SUMMARY

> This poem is an analysis of man's two-fold nature (matter and spirit) and his natural fortune of birth, death-in-sex, and rebirth in poetry.

Analysis. Part one records that "I" (Thomas) is intricately composed of metal body (minerals) and spirit (ghost), beginning with doom in the penis and doom in the spirit to fuse mortality and immortality. Thomas re-composes this parallel miracle in his poetry by indicating man's activities. Part two indicates that "they" (Thomas' intricate images) record the elements of nature and the doom-in-sex of man. Part three continues the thematic statement of the intricate images' recording of the mystery of death-in-love and death-in-life.

Form And Style. This poem is arranged in three parts containing six **stanzas** of six lines each. Each stanza is composed of long and short lines by means of which the rhythm rises and falls. The **rhyme** is based on the terminal letters of each line (near-rhyme) in the pattern of abaaba. Internal **assonance**, particularly of o's and i's, and the use of terminal "l" sounds in most lines indicate Thomas' concern with tonal qualities.

THIS BREAD I BREAK

Introduction. This poem was composed on December 24, 1933, but it was revised in 1936 for its publication in the July 16, 1936 issue of *New English Weekly*. It later appeared in *Twenty-five Poems*.

SUMMARY

> "This Bread I Break" is a short poem which depicts the sacramental communion of God, man, and nature.

Analysis. The sacramental bread and wine were once part of nature, but either man or wind destroyed the crops. Once the sap-blood coursed through the grape's vine and the oat was happy in the wind, but man destroyed the sun (= Son) and pulled the wind down. The flesh and blood that are symbolized in the eucharist were once oat and grape, living members of nature, which man now destroys.

Form And Style. This poem, composed of three five-line stanzas, has occasional **rhyme** or no rhyme (except for the terminal **couplet**). The length of each line in a **stanza** varies according to its position, the first and last lines are the longest, the third line the shortest, the second and fourth lines vary in length: four-stress, three or four-stress, two-stress, three or four-stress, four-stress.

INCARNATE DEVIL

Introduction. This poem, originally entitled "Poem for Sunday," was composed on May 16, 1933, and published in the *Sunday Referee* of August 11, 1935. It was revised on January 20, 1936, and published in *Twenty-five Poems*.

SUMMARY

Using the **imagery** of the Garden of Eden and the Fall of Man, Thomas attacks a weak and ineffectual God who condemned sex as devilish and praised abstinence as divine.

Analysis. In the Garden of Eden during the season of reproduction and gestation in nature, the serpent presented the bearded apple (the fruit of knowledge and the knowledge of genitalia) and God wandered as a warden in a prison, playing pardons on his fiddle. Creation is the product, not of God alone, but of God and the devil together. Both Christian and pagan mythology reflect the same archetypal myth - the union of evil and good in the Garden of Eden which resulted in man's imprisonment in life and his freedom in sexual creativity.

Form And Style. This poem is composed of three **stanzas** of six lines, rhyming abacbc deedff gghhii in near-rhyme. **Assonance** within the lines is prominent.

TO-DAY, THIS INSECT

Introduction. "To-day, This Insect" was composed on December 18, 1930, but was revised in 1936. It appeared in *Purpose for the Winter*, 1936 issue, and in *Twenty-five Poems*.

SUMMARY

The life cycle of an insect, paralleled by sexual **imagery**, is essentially an analysis of poetic creativity.

Analysis. Now that Thomas' poetry has achieved some standing he divides his **theme** between the themes of womb-tomb and birth and development. The story of the Garden of Eden, indicated in the first **stanza**, is developed in the second in sexual terms of copulation, orgasm and gestation. In the third **stanza** the death aspect of his **themes** is developed at length, and Thomas reaffirms that man will be his **metaphor**. His poetry is, thus, a statement presented on intricate parallel levels of the creation, and process toward death of the universe, the child, and his poetry.

Form And Style. The **rhyme**, if there is any, is perhaps approximate. The most obvious stylistic achievement is the reversal of images in the single lines following the first and second stanzas. The length of the lines varies, as does the rhythm, in the typical manner of Thomas.

THE SEED-AT-ZERO

Introduction. This mediocre poem was composed on August 29, 1933, but revised in 1936 for its inclusion in the *Twenty-five Poems* volume. The earlier version can be found in the November, 1955 issue of *Poetry*.

SUMMARY

> "The Seed-at-Zero" is a restatement of Thomas' womb-tomb thesis of the futility of sexual reproduction.

Analysis. The chief problem of this poem is determining just what the seed-at-zero represents. Presented in images of human sperm and plant seed, the major characteristic of the seed is its inability to fertilize. The difficulty is in deciding whether the infertility arises from a natural conflict of internal potent and sterile forces or from the external use of contraceptives. Derek Stanford thinks that the seed-at-zero represents "man with his vital forces spent." Elder Olson declares a positive interpretation, based on Thomas' use of military **imagery**, of the seed at the zero hour ready to attack. Professor Clark Emery thinks that the poem "moves forward, stating the conditions of birth, pleading for the possibility of growth, and indicating the status of man in depth."

Form And Style. The eight **stanzas** are written in pairs, the last word of each even-numbered **stanza** (with one exception) is the same word as its equivalent in the preceding **stanza**. The last three lines of each even-numbered **stanzas** repeat the last three lines of the previous stanza, and the first three lines echo the preceding first three lines.

BRIGHT NOTES STUDY GUIDE

SHALL GODS BE SAID TO THUMP THE CLOUDS

Introduction. This poem was composed in August, 1933 and revised about 1936. It was first published in *Twenty-five Poems*.

SUMMARY

> Thomas questions that natural phenomena are caused by anthropomorphic gods who are represented by stone statues. Are these gods? Yet these representations are the closest man has come to depicting divinity.

Analysis. Thomas takes examples from foul weather and asks if storms and rain can be said to be caused by gods. But the gods are stone images, and can stone drum or chime? Thomas concludes with the order (jussive subjunctive) to let the stones speak in a universal tongue.

Form And Style. The four **stanzas** are structured or constructed of 4-3-3-4 lines. The first three **stanzas** are composed of interrogatives; the final **stanza** contains initial and terminal short imperative sentences and a middle interrogative sentence. The first three **stanzas** begin with four questions which are answered by the first line of the fourth **stanza**. There are four stresses to the lines. The **rhyme** is near-rhyme, with occasionally unusual rhyme.

HERE IN THIS SPRING

Introduction. This poem, composed on July 9, 1933, was revised in January, 1936, for publication in *Twenty-five Poems*.

SUMMARY

> Another statement of the ever-present **theme** that life is a process of dying.

Analysis. The various signs and symbols of the four seasons are only signals of the process of time which leads all things to maturity and death. Thomas should be able to tell the season by the signs, but the worm and slug tell time better because they destroy. The intimations of precarious mortality are quite obvious.

Form And Style. The poem is composed of two quatrains, a **stanza** of five lines, and another quatrain. The near-rhyme of consonants is in the pattern of abba cdcd eefff ghgh.

DO YOU NOT FATHER ME

Introduction. "Do You Not Father Me" was composed about 1935. It appeared first in the *Scottish Bookman of October*, 1935, and then in *Twenty-five Poems*.

SUMMARY

> Another womb-tomb, creation-destruction poem, relating man to the universe.

Analysis. In a series of questions Thomas seeks to find his identity. He asks if "you" did not father, mother, sister, brother, him; if he himself is not also father, mother, sister, brother, etc.;

if he was not fathered in a process of destruction; and, finally, if he also will carry on the process of destruction in his identity of creator.

Form And Style. All the poetic techniques of **alliteration**, assonance and **consonance** are here in this poem of four stanzas, thirty-two lines, with four stresses to the line. The approximate **rhyme** is in an ababcdcd pattern.

OUT OF THE SIGHS

Introduction. This poem was composed on June 7, 1932. It was revised about 1936 and appeared in *Twenty-five Poems*.

SUMMARY

"Out of the Sighs" is a description of painful emotions.

Analysis. After some tragic event in the life of seventeen-year-old Thomas, grief and agony come; then the spirit reasserts itself and tries to forget the disappointment of perpetual defeat, perhaps in love. The one who has no regrets will ache too long because he is too self-centered. But if it were enough to feel regret for a wasted love and reassure oneself by lies, he could bear the suffering and be cured. But if such rationalization were really enough to cure the agony and regret, the lover could not have been a genuine lover but more of a lusting dog.

Form And Style. This poem is an excellent sharing, not merely an analysis or description, of a painful emotion. The poem is effective because the sense of the feelings predominates rather than the usual intellectual generalizations. "Out of the Sighs" is written in four **stanzas** of nine, seven, seven, and six lines, in free verse.

HOLD HARD, THESE ANCIENT MINUTES IN THE CUCKOO'S MONTH

Introduction. This poem was composed early in 1936, and was first published in *Caravel* for March of that year. It was subsequently published in *Twenty-five Poems*.

SUMMARY

Time is a process of nature (or nature is a process of time) wherein springtime rides in a steeplechase into the summer.

Analysis. Time is a rider, and Thomas addresses the country in May to prepare for the processes of nature which are like a steeplechase proceeding across the land. Time is a destructive force, like the hawk, which upsets seasons and overturns the land.

Form And Style. The four six-line **stanzas** are written in blank verse. Most of the lines contain five beats, but some lines exceed this number. There is occasional assonance.

WAS THERE A TIME

Introduction. Composed on February 8, 1933, and revised in December, 1935, "Was There a Time" first appeared in the *New English Weekly* of September 3, 1936. It was then published in *Twenty-five Poems*.

SUMMARY

> Time, the process of life, is also the destroyer of life.

Analysis. The poem opens with a question, asking if there was ever a time when circus dancers could avoid their troubles. But time is like a maggot and no one is safe. Ignorance is the only wisdom, just as the cleanest hands are those that belong to people without arms. A knowledge of time brings a knowledge of the destructive course of time, therefore ignorance is the best and happiest form of being.

Form And Style. This short, nine-line poem has nothing of particular value in it. It is an example of the juvenile Thomas stamping a **theme** to death. There is a consonantal near-rhyme of aabbccxdd.

NOW

Introduction. "Now" was composed about 1935 and was first published in *Twenty-five Poems*.

SUMMARY

> The poem is a command to say "nay" to death and to quietly accept death.

Analysis. If one should, without anger, accept the dust of death, forsake him. Say no to the yes query of death. Deny, or do not say, that the dead will rise again. Say no to that form of science which deadens one's sense of the mystery of life. Thomas concludes with disdain for the theory or myth of the apocalypse or the spiritual soul liberated by death. Man is as mysterious in his own right, Thomas says, as the air, the blood, the penis, or the cloud.

Form And Style. "Now" is a very obscure and syntactically difficult poem. There are five **stanzas** of seven lines each. The first two lines are repeated in each **stanza**; the first four lines of every stanza are based on adding one syllable to the previous line's syllabication. The fourth and sixth, fifth and seventh lines contain near-rhyme.

WHY EAST WIND CHILLS

Introduction. This poem was written on July 1, 1933, and revised on January 21, 1936. It was published in the *New English Weekly* of July 16, 1936, and *Twenty-five Poems*.

SUMMARY

> Since there is no answer to the "why?" questions of children until after death, it is best, therefore, to be content with not knowing.

Analysis. To all the many questions of children, "why does Jack Frost come?," "why does the East Wind chill?," "why...," etc., Thomas hears only the voice of the stars saying, "be content" and "know no answer." Although modern science knows most things, the questions of children are still (and always) impossible to answer until after death.

Form And Style. Apparently haphazard, the structure of the poem re-inforces the uncertainty of the **theme**. Just as answers to the children's questions are, at best, uncertain, so the style and structure of the poem appear uncertain. The three **stanzas** are of uneven length: nine, six, and eleven lines. There is no **rhyme**, but many terminal words end in the same letter. There is occasional **assonance** and **alliteration**. The length of the individual lines also varies between four and three stresses.

A GRIEF AGO

Introduction. This poem was composed about 1935 and first published in *Programme* for October 23, 1935. It was subsequently published in *Twenty-five Poems*.

SUMMARY

> A very obscure poem that has been variously interpreted as an embryo speaking to its mother or as Thomas speaking to Caitlin.

Analysis. In sexual **imagery** obviously describing the sex act in progress, Thomas describes the woman who was who he holds and who is his grief and who lies on field and sand. The fourth **stanza** questions who she is, and declares that the sea drives on her and shapes her children with the voice of water. The final **stanza** is clearly phallic. Thomas tells her to breathe-in her dead through the sea of sperm, that is, unite her past and future history as an archetypal mother image. Let her close her fist against the treacherous eyes of the dead in the grave.

Form And Style. "A Grief Ago" is written in five eight-line stanzas. The first, fourth, sixth and last lines of each **stanza** are short, that is, containing two-stresses. The other lines are four-stressed. The near-rhyme is in an abcabddc pattern. **Alliteration**, **assonance**, and **consonance** assist the tonal quality of the poem and reinforce the **theme** by enriching the meaning through sound.

HOW SOON THE SERVANT SUN

Introduction. Written about 1935, this poem appeared with "A Grief Ago" in *Programme* on October 23, 1935. It was then printed in *Twenty-five Poems*.

SUMMARY

Using the image of embryonic development Thomas questions the riddle of time and indicates that he will poetically trumpet the answer.

Analysis. How soon the sun, the servant and marker of Time, can move time to develop the embryo from an egg to fetus with umbilical cord, Sir morrow tells you. The embryo develops further, trapped in its shroud, and finally breaks into the light. He can see in the womb that life and death are synonymous; he cries, and hell blasts back the trumpeting answering voice.

Form And Style. The primary quality of this short, five-stanza poem is **assonance**. There is occasional **alliteration**. Each **stanza** contains seven lines, with occasional rhyme.

BRIGHT NOTES STUDY GUIDE

EARS IN THE TURRETS HEAR

Introduction. This poem was written on July 17, 1933, and revised about 1936. It did not appear in print until its publication in *Twenty-five Poems*.

SUMMARY

> "Ears In the Turrets Hear" is Thomas' analysis of his fear of involvement with mankind, particularly with those who might hurt him. In this poem he wrestles with the question, "Is engagement or disengagement the more satisfactory mode of living?"

Analysis. Upstairs, Thomas' ears hear and his eyes see someone at the front door. He asks if he should open the door or remain a recluse all his life. And he asks if the hands outside come in hostility or friendship. Even if he lived on an island out of sight of the mainland, ships would anchor in the bay. He would have to ask himself again if he should welcome the sailors or remain aloof. He concludes by reiterating his initial question, "do the hands of the stranger at the door and the holds of the ships in the bay contain hostility or friendship?"

Form And Style. This poem is written in four **stanzas** of varying length and a concluding **couplet**. The first and third **stanzas** are comprised of nine lines, the second **stanza** of seven lines, and the fourth stanza of six lines. The **rhyme** is intricate, based on **assonance**, with many terminal words repeated throughout. The individual lines contain six syllables, except for the last line of the first and third stanzas, and the first line of the couplet.

FOSTER THE LIGHT

Introduction. "Foster the Light" was composed on February 2, 1934, and published in the *Sunday Referee* of October 28, 1934. It was revised about 1936 and published in *Contemporary Poetry & Prose* of May, 1936. The revised version appeared in *Twenty-five Poems*.

SUMMARY

This poem is an exhortation to Thomas the poet to master all the forces of life and nature and to produce the shapes of poetry.

Analysis. "Foster the Light" was composed on Feb-moon. Weather only the wind that strips the marrow from the bone. Master and conquer the night but do not serve the cold intellect. Become a farmer of the seasons and nature and include them in your poetry. Do not become a hoot-owl in the dark but rail out against sentimentality and superstitious religion. Take your poetic music from nature. In the fourth **stanza** Thomas addresses the sea, telling it not to sorrow when his poetry is phallic (the sea is a life-force, the phallus is a force of death and destruction). The fifth **stanza** addresses the life-force itself, inviting it to make the world of the poet as the poet has made a manshape of the world.

Form And Style. Rhyming (generally) aabccb, this poem is written in five six-line stanzas. The length of the lines varies, but each line contains four stresses. The rhyme-scheme is based on **assonance** and consonance. **Assonance** and **alliteration** are evidenced throughout.

THE HAND THAT SIGNED THE PAPER

Introduction. "The Hand That Signed the Paper" was composed on August 17, 1933, but it was revised in 1935 before it appeared in *New Verse* for December of that year. It was subsequently published in *Twenty-five Poems*.

SUMMARY

A dehumanized hand, without passion or feeling, signs a peace treaty and just as aloofly begins war.

Analysis. The hand that signed a paper also destroyed a city by signing a declaration of war. The five fingers royal in their ability, killed a monarch. The same hand, however, that declared war and killed has put an end to war and murder by signing a peace treaty. But the hand that signed a treaty also bred famine and further destruction. The power of the hand is great, but it does not feel pity or compassion.

Form And Style. The poem is simply constructed, four quatrains rhyming with true **rhyme** abab. Each **stanza** begins with a parallel reference to the hand. Even the meter is in the familiar iambs.

SHOULD LANTERNS SHINE

Introduction. "Should Lanterns Shine" was composed possibly sometime between July, 1932, and January, 1933. It was revised about 1935 and appeared in *New Verse* along with "The Hand That Signed the Paper." It was published in *Twenty-five Poems*.

THE MAJOR POEMS

SUMMARY

> An illustration of the emptiness and uselessness of a religious belief which is lost in the light of reason.

Analysis. If a lantern should shine on religion and faith, religion would wither away. Religion is a human organization based on humanity's private needs and fears of the dark; therefore exposure to light would show it to be a painted corpse. Thomas has also been told that religious assent is an irrational or emotional assent, not a rational one. But even so, religion has not been effective. Thomas concludes in an enigmatic couplet that the process that started when he was a child (either religious doubt or the vocation of poesy) has not yet terminated.

Form And Style. The poem is written in a **stanza** of eight lines, one of seven lines, and two self-contained couplets. It is in **free verse**, with the stresses varying from three to four per line.

I HAVE LONGED TO MOVE AWAY

Introduction. This poem was composed on March 1, 1933, and revised probably on January 13, 1935. It appeared in *New Verse* for December, 1935, and in *Twenty-five Poems*.

SUMMARY

> Time, which steals composure and confidence ritualistic Christian religion, but he is afraid. Yet he does not wish to die hypocritically following a convention.

Analysis. Thomas has longed to abandon the worn-out lie and the fear of the unknown that has grown more terrible and terrifying with the passage of time. He has longed to move away from the belief in ghosts in the air, from the meaningless repetition of formulas, and from the noise of vocal prayer and songs. He has longed to abandon faith but he is afraid lest there be "some life in the old boy yet." He shall not live by the conventional tokens of tipped hats in greeting or kisses exchanged over the phone or by fear of the dark unknown at night. He would not desire to live by these because they are half **convention** (a tradition carried on even though the meaning has been lost) and half lie.

Form And Style. The poem is divided into two **stanzas** of ten lines each, the first **stanza** stating Thomas' objections, the second his fears. The rhyme is near-rhyme, based on **assonance**. It is a pattern of abbabacddc effegghhii.

FIND MEAT ON BONES

Introduction. "Find Meat on Bones" was composed on July 15, 1993 and revised January, 1936. It was first published in the Spring, 1936, issue of *Purpose* and later in *Twenty-five Poems*.

SUMMARY

> A dialogue between a father, who advises a sensual approach to life (carpe diem), and a son, who has tried his father's advice and rejected it.

Analysis. The first two **stanzas** present the father's advice: take advantage of youth to drink and enjoy a sexual life before old age takes away the blossom of your conquests; rebel against religious dictatorship and the dictatorship of time, rebel against the process of decay. The second two **stanzas** present the son's reply: the son has tried his father's sensual approach to life and it has almost physically destroyed him; he cannot deny the process of life, even though time is a destroying maggot, for there is beauty in time. The final **stanza** recapitulates the previous positions but unifies them: the heavens and seas still rule and are strong, but light and dark, life and death, creation and destruction are a unity. He rejects his father's advice to war against destiny and doom.

Form And Style. The poem is composed in four eight-line **stanzas** and a final nine-line **stanza**. The near **rhyme** is arranged in patterns: the father's and son's **stanzas rhyme** abbbccab abxbaaab, and the final stanza **rhymes** abbbaaaab. The fifth line of every **stanza** except the fourth stanza is short; in the fourth **stanza** the sixth line is short. Every fifth line ends a sentence.

GRIEF THIEF OF TIME

Introduction. This poem was written on August 26, 1933, and was published in the February, 1936, issue of *Comment* and in *Twenty-five Poems*.

SUMMARY

> The process of time, wherein life is but a journey to death, ironically acts against itself because the old forget sex, the cause of new deaths being brought into the world.

Analysis. Time, which steals composure and confidence because of the fear of death and awareness of the process of death, is overcome by the old because they have forgotten grief and doubt, and can no longer perform the sex act. Time, a stud producing new lives to participate in the process of death, is outwitted because the genitals of the old are impotent. Time has carried them on to the point that his destructive purpose is defeated.

Form And Style. The two **stanzas** of this poem contain fourteen lines each. The punctuation is difficult and the rhyme-scheme (of near-rhyme) is also difficult because of the use of **assonance** in near-rhyme: ababbaaababba ababacdcdcdaca. **Assonance** and internal **rhyme** can be found in the verses.

AND DEATH SHALL HAVE NO DOMINION

Introduction. "And Death Shall Have No Dominion," one of Thomas' best known works, was composed in April, 1933, and published in the *New English Weekly* the following May 18th. It was revised in February, 1936, and included *Twenty-five Poems*.

SUMMARY

In this poem Thomas denies that death shall conquer man because, after death, man will become part of nature and nature's life-forces.

Analysis. Death shall have no dominion because dead men will be united with nature in the wind and the sky. Even though lovers die, love shall not die. Death shall have no dominion because the dead will no longer suffer pain, faith, or evil. Death shall have no dominion because, although man can no longer enjoy the beauties of nature, he shall be part of nature.

Form And Style. The poem is composed of three **stanzas** of nine lines each (symbolically appropriate in a poem such as this: three equals the Trinity or Supreme Architect of the world, nine is the perfect number). Each **stanza** begins and ends with the title. Each stanza is "rhymed" on the basis of the terminal sound, aaaabaaba. The length of the lines are generally **tetrameter** (iambic) with occasionally hendecasyllabic (eleven) lines.

THEN WAS MY NEOPHYTE

Introduction. This poem was possibly composed between July, 1932, and January, 1933. It was revised about 1936 and appeared in the October-December, 1936, issue of *Purpose*. It was published in *Twenty-five Poems*.

SUMMARY

> Time, with life as a process of death, is again a murderer. The emptiness (vanity) of life refutes religious propaganda for an afterlife.

Analysis. At a certain time Thomas' religious initiate, his child, walked on its knees in the sea. Like a hermaphrodite snail, and the evolution of animals, the child eventually achieved a life on land. The child grew, developed in time and became a social animal. Time, throughout all these periods, was less than God. But the grown child now realized that God was a myth, a false photograph. God's part in the mystery of life is as real as a motion picture. Thomas asks who stops his story, his life. God answers with a question, "Who could kill you since there is a mysterious and mystical afterlife?" Thomas replies that Time is killing him. Again God denies that Time could kill him, but Thomas saw Time murder him.

Form And Style. Each of the four **stanzas** is in two parts, each part is a sentence. The **rhyme** reinforces this division, the first part (six lines) **rhymes** abcbca, the second part (six lines) rhymes adedea. Equivalent lines in each **stanza** have similar length. There is little **alliteration**, but there is assonance.

ALTARWISE BY OWL-LIGHT

Introduction. The first seven **sonnets** were composed about 1935 and appeared in the December, 1935, issue of *Life & Letters Today*. The eighth to tenth **sonnets** were written the following year. The eighth sonnet appeared in the May, 1936, issue of *Contemporary Poetry & Prose*, and the ninth and tenth **sonnets** appeared in the July, 1936, issue. All ten sonnets were published in *Twenty-five Poems*.

SUMMARY

> These ten **sonnets** record Thomas' development from embryo to poet.

Analysis. The first **sonnet** shows Thomas in the womb recalling his conception and initiation into the destructive process of time (womb-tomb). In the second **sonnet** the embryo has become formed in the womb and breaks out of it in birth into death. The third **sonnet** shows Thomas' youth and early interest in sex. By the time of the fourth **sonnet** Thomas has grown to that age of childhood which asks questions about sex, the meaning of life, death, and the passing of time. In the fifth **sonnet** the boy, older now, is playing at games and grows to question the validity of Christianity. There is a hint of adolescent masturbation. The sixth **sonnet** shows Thomas' initial creativity with words (poetry) and sex. In the seventh **sonnet** Thomas declares that Time, couched in sexual language, will be his **theme**. Thomas equates, in the eighth **sonnet**, poetic creativity and Christ's crucifixion, since the result of both will be a universal message. In the ninth sonnet the crucified one is mummified and resurrected in the desert; Thomas' poems are printed and mummified in libraries, yet the **theme** of death will be resurrected and sent forth on their messianic voyage. The tenth sonnet declares that Thomas' poetry will replace the Gospels as guideposts for life's voyage.

Form And Style. Although written in the **sonnet** form of fourteen lines, the punctuation and **rhyme** breaks down into a sestet-octave division instead of the customary octave-sestet (eight and six). The **rhyme** scheme is in the form of abcbac / dede / fgfg. Punctuation also reinforces the division by **rhyme**: in every **sonnet** except the seventh there is a major punction pause at the sixth line. Every **sonnet** except the first and fifth also has a major pause at the tenth line. The meter is sprung, that is, there are four-stresses to the line, common in Thomas.

QUESTIONS ON TWENTY-FIVE POEMS

Question. What are the main **themes** in these poems?

Answer. Thomas has again declared the futility of sexual reproduction because life remains for him a cycle to destruction and death. He has attacked the Christian myths and proclaimed a sacramental union of God-man-and-nature, and involved an analysis of poetic creativity in terms of sexual intercourse and embryonic development. He also indicates a distrust of reason, and shows the life-force leading to death but also overcoming it, and reaffirms life.

Question. Has there been any change in Thomas' technique?

Answer. The poems of this volume continue to be the outbursts of a boily boy in love with the shape and sounds of words, obscure in their ambiguous symbolism and **syntax**, with constant repetition of womb and tomb, phallic signs and wearisome attitudes.

MAJOR POEMS

THE MAP OF LOVE

BECAUSE THE PLEASURE-BIRD WHISTLES

Introduction. This poem was composed in January, 1939, and published in *Twentieth-Century Verse* the following month. It was the opening poem of *The Map of Love* volume of verse.

SUMMARY

Modern life, in snowy London at New Year's, is as sinful as Sodom, but Thomas will not refuse to look back at it because the past serves the present.

Analysis. On a snowy New Year's night (the poem's original title was "January, 1939") a love-sick man sits alone in his room. The storm outside is like a shower of drugs or goose feathers, but inside the man considers the story of Lot's wife (who looked back) in Sodom. Because song-birds can be made to whistle and sing better if they are blinded, shall a horse that is blind sing better? Because Lot's wife looked back on past sin and savoured the unnatural sex practices of Sodom, shall Thomas not look back at the life of the past year? Thomas furnishes the story of Lot's wife and destroyed (or damned) Sodom-London with the meat of a myth and over this past meal repeats a present blessing.

Form And Style. This poem of twenty-five lines of **free verse** was occasioned by a visit Thomas made to London in December, 1938. The free verse is broken occasionally by irregular **rhyme**. The images are intricately structured, but they are chiefly snow, Sodom, and dinner.

I MAKE THIS IN A WARRING ABSENCE

Introduction. Originally titled "Poem to Caitlin" and then "Poem (for Caitlin)," "I Make This In a Warring Absence" was composed in November, 1937. It was published in the January-February, 1938, issue of *Twentieth Century Verse* and in *The Map of Love*.

SUMMARY

> This poem records the effects of a domestic quarrel.

Analysis. Thomas is writing this poem after a tumultuous quarrel with Caitlin when her desire for love-making has turned cold and she refused him. Her pride has made her absent herself from him and underlined her contraries the contradictions in her makeup - that she could love sex so much, yet spurn it out of pride because of a quarrel. Thomas walked the seashore, thinking angrily about her biting words, but he returned and obtained her forgiveness. Now, in the calm of sexual return, Thomas is writing this poem in the presence of the forgiving Caitlin.

Form And Style. This poem is composed of nine **stanzas** of alternating eight and seven lines. The rhyme-scheme is intricately built upon **assonance** and **consonance**. The majority of the lines end in m's or n's, s sounds, or in d's.

WHEN ALL MY FIVE AND COUNTRY SENSES SEE

Introduction. This poem was probably composed in the period between July, 1932, and January, 1933. It was revised in 1938 and appeared in the August issue of *Poetry*, and later published in *The Map of Love*.

SUMMARY

A manifesto of poetic intent, **theme** and method.

Analysis. Reminiscent of Bottom's "The eye of man hath not heard, the ear of man hath not seen" in *A Midsummer-Night's Dream*, Thomas' five senses are so unified that they share one another's functions. His five senses are like eyes commanded by the poetic heart. They will see Love pared and wintered in the cold by the stars and washed away at the beach; they will see the tongue cry that the female organs are repaired and sewed. When the senses sleep and no longer see, the heart (which is sensual) will observe.

Form And Style. Divided into a ten-line **stanza** and a quatrain, this poem is similarly divided by **rhyme** and thematic statement. The rhyme-scheme is ababacaac dede. The first **stanza** presents the result of the conditional "when" all Thomas' senses see. The quatrain is more of a statement of the heart's capabilities when the condition of the first **stanza** is negated.

BRIGHT NOTES STUDY GUIDE

WE LYING BY SEASAND

Introduction. "We Lying by Seasand" was composed on May 16, 1933. It was revised sometime during or after 1936, for it appeared in the January, 1937, issue of *Poetry* in its present form. It was published in *The Map of Love*.

SUMMARY

> This poem is a mocking of the threat of impending war in Europe and a hope, immediately rejected, that it will blow away.

Analysis. We who lie on the seashore mock those who follow the rivers of blood. This beach scene is a shallow grave and we can hear on the wind the calls on both sides of the channel that follow the colors. There is a sense of hurry in the sound of the grains of sand going by, although the tide is quiet. We hope that the wind will blow away the sand and blood-colored rock, but wishes are impotent and we cannot stop the arrival of the weather-breaking rock.

Form And Style. The rhyme-scheme of this twenty-four-line poem begins in an easy abab form, but soon becomes intricate and convoluted. The rhythm is carried by four-stress lines which occasionally drop to three-stress lines and terminate in five-stress lines. **Alliteration**, **assonance**, and internal **rhyme** are unable to raise this poem above the level of virtuoso craftsmanship.

IT IS THE SINNER'S DUST-TONGUED BELL

Introduction. This poem was composed about 1936. It was first published in *Twentieth Century Verse* for January, 1937, and later in *The Map of Love*.

Analysis. "It Is the Sinner's Dust-tongued Bell" is a poem on the griefs and adjustments early in marriage, with implications of Thomas' participating in the womb-tomb process again.

SUMMARY

The sinner's bell, dusty from disuse, calls Thomas to church where Time presides at a black mass. Personified processes of time are also there. Time and death participate in the process of creation, just as summer will be followed by winter. The final **stanza** limits the locale to the Thomas' marriage bed, where a divine service of intercourse takes place (intercourse parallels the divine Creation) and produces the grief and sin of a black mass (intercourse produces life, which is eventually death).

Form And Style. This poem is composed of five six-line **stanzas** which **rhyme** abcabc. Each third and sixth line is short, containing four stresses. The long lines contain five or more stresses.

O MAKE ME A MASK

Introduction. "O Make Me a Mask" was composed about March 31, 1933, and revised in November, 1937. It was published in *Poetry* in August, 1938, and in *Life & Letters Today* the following month. It appeared in *The Map of Love*.

SUMMARY

Thomas prays for a protective mask and armor against inquisitive and bothersome scrutiny.

Analysis. Thomas prays for a mask or wall to hide the rebellion in his expression from the sharp eyes of outsiders, and a gag to silence the stabbing tongues of his enemies. He also wishes for the appearance of a dunce to protect his brain from those who would examine it, and the mask of grief so that he can examine others who try to hide their losses by feigned smiles and laughter.

Form And Style. This short poem of twelve long lines rhymes abcacacdefef. Every line contains **assonance**, **consonance** and some alliteration.

THE SPIRE CRANES

Introduction. "The Spire Cranes" was written on January 27, 1931, when Thomas was sixteen years old, and revised in November, 1937. It appeared in *Wales* in March 1938, *Poetry* in August, 1938, and in *The Map of Love*.

SUMMARY

The dogmatism of organized churches imprisons the naturally free birds, but the sound of the bells moves freely away from it. Thomas exhorts himself to remain free of religion.

Analysis. The spire stretches toward heaven. The carved stone statues of birds on it, birds which should be able to fly freely, are not able to be hurt by falling, but are not able to be free. The spire has imprisoned in stone the spirit of something free. But the music of the church chimes escapes the prison. Thomas advises himself not to let himself be imprisoned by the road of the prodigal's return, but to remain free as music and be a poet.

Form And Style. This short, eleven-line poem begins with two sentences in its first line. The next two sentences end in the middle of lines, and line eight even contains the end of one sentence and another complete sentence. The **rhyme** scheme is aabbccdddee. **Assonance**, **alliteration** and **consonance** are evident throughout.

AFTER THE FUNERAL (IN MEMORY OF ANN JONES)

Introduction. This poem was composed on February 10, 1933, and revised in March, 1938. It was published in the Summer, 1938, issue of *Life & Letters Today* and in *The Map of Love*.

SUMMARY

"After the Funeral" is an **elegy** to Thomas' ancient peasant aunt, Ann Jones, whose instinctive love and virtue Thomas uses to satirize hypocritical religion.

Analysis. After the funeral, the graveside services are like the brays of mules, the conventional and hypocritical sorrow is as empty of value and sincerity as the words of a mule. Thomas stands alone with Ann Jones, whose love was fertile for all Wales (although such **imagery** is greatly out of proportion for her; she makes no Celtic priest of her body). Thomas calls all nature to join in the funeral service, for Ann loved nature. She was meek, but the stone memorial is giant. Her humble, housewife hands are cramped with daily tasks and with religion.

The external, bizarre, and insincere service and memorial storm over Thomas until the animals cry "love" and the plants lay seeds on the grave mound.

Form And Style. The forty lines of this **elegy** are an excellent example of Thomas' ability with the sound of words. In fact, the poem should be heard and not read (this holds true for all Thomas' verse), and it is fortunate that a recording of Thomas reading this poem is available. The **rhyme** is generally of an alternating **assonance** or **consonance**, the tonal quality reinforced by internal alliteration.

ONCE IT WAS THE COLOUR OF SAYING

Introduction. This poem was possibly composed in the period between July, 1932, and January, 1933. It was revised in December, 1938, and published in *Wales*, March, 1939. It appeared in *The Map of Love*.

SUMMARY

> Thomas states the necessity of revising his approach to poetry.

Analysis. Once Thomas' poetry soaked his writing table with the uglier aspects of childhood and growth, knowledge and sex. Now he must undo those sayings. (He recalls in childhood that he and his friends would sneak up on lovers lying in the park at night and throw stones at them.) Their language had many shades and was like lightning. But now he must cast off the writing of memories and wind off every stone that he threw like a reel.

Form And Style. Rhyming abbacbdceedab, this thirteenline poem contains lines of irregular length. It is a manifesto of Thomas' intention to return to poetic integrity, but it contains little of universal value beyond that.

NOT FROM THIS ANGER

Introduction. "Not From This Anger" was composed on April 20, 1933, and revised January, 1938. It was published in the August, 1938, issue of *Poetry* and in *The Map of Love*.

SUMMARY

Thomas has been refused sexual relations by Caitlin and has become angry, but now he realizes that giving way to angry outbursts is an unsatisfactory way of behaving.

Analysis. Not from anger shall Caitlin receive weeds and hunger, because her loins refused intercourse and Thomas became impotent. Her refusal to have intercourse and subsequent making up shall not cause him to inwardly burn. Thomas has matured enough to realize that the ups and downs of marital (or martial) life should not affect one permanently.

Form And Style. The rhyme-scheme is odd and difficult to interpret in this fourteen-line poem. It is certainly not in the traditional scheme of the **sonnet**, but is more aababcc / aac / aaac. The seventh, eleventh and fourteenth lines are short.

BRIGHT NOTES STUDY GUIDE

HOW SHALL MY ANIMAL

Introduction. This poem was composed on December 9, 1930, and is the earliest poem in Thomas' notebooks. It was revised in March, 1938, and published in the October issue of *Criterion*. It appeared in *The Map of Love*.

SUMMARY

> This poem asks how Thomas can prevent the loss of his creative fury when poetry is put down on paper.

Analysis. How shall my creation, whose magical shape I trace inside my head, endure burial under a construction of words, with a dust-jacket veil at its head; who should be angry and argue with the elements of the outside world? How shall my animal fervor be able to magnetize and attract melting male and female to love, labor and kill in the exhilarating bursting of sexual intercourse? I shall not be able to fish and angle or to clasp the fury of sexual activity. The final **stanza** is an address to the poem, cold as clay, dead and frozen, to sigh and rest. Even though the creative energy has been robbed, the animal (creative imagination) had kicked and leaped in the head and dug its grave in the poet's heart.

Form And Style. "How Shall My Animal" is composed of four eleven-line stanzas. The first two stanzas each contain an interrogative sentence, the third **stanza** a declarative sentence, and the fourth stanza two imperative sentences. The tonal quality of internal **assonance** and **consonance** is more important than terminal **rhyme**, which appears and disappears. Internal rhyme and the varying length of the lines add to the rhythm created by the sound of the words.

THE MAJOR POEMS

THE TOMBSTONE TOLD WHEN SHE DIED

Introduction. "The Tombstone Told When She Died" was composed in July, 1933, revised in September, 1938, and published in the Winter edition of *Seven*. It appeared in *The Map of Love* volume of Thomas' verse.

SUMMARY

This poem is a play on the meaning of the word "die" as sexual intercourse and physical death. A virgin who has married but died before sexual consummation of the marriage could occur nevertheless imagined that her death pangs were the pains of the penetration of her husband's penis.

Analysis. Thomas has stopped at a certain tombstone one rainy day and read that a married virgin lies there, died before Thomas was conceived in his mother's womb. In town he further learns the events of her death-bed: beforehand or penis could enter her she cried that she was naked in bed and suffering the pains of intercourse and love. Her delirium was as factual as a fictitious movie, she died before the newlyweds could make love and the pain in her womb was caused by disease and not intercourse.

Form And Style. The poem is composed of one **stanza** of thirty lines, three stresses in a line. Its **rhyme** is complex and difficult to work out.

ON NO WORK OF WORDS

Introduction. This poem was written about February 16, 1933, and revised in September, 1938. It appeared in the *Wales* publication of March, 1939, and in *The Map of Love*.

SUMMARY

> "On No Work of Words" records a period of aridity during which Thomas is unable to write, yet refuses to abandon his poetic integrity and recopy previous themes.

Analysis. Thomas has been unable to write for three months and begins to criticize his poverty and talent. He rejects the temptation to fall back on linguistic gifts which brought others money. To copy the treasures of others is a pleasant thought but will bring death to his own style of poetry. He rejects surrender and refuses to give up his poetic vocation.

Form And Style. Written in four contained tercets, the rhyme-scheme carries the poem forward by continuing the **rhyme**, almost in the manner of terza rima: aab ccb dde ffe. The rhythm is the expected sprung rhythm with its foundation in the number of stresses per line.

A SAINT ABOUT TO FALL

Introduction. Originally titled "Poem in the Ninth Month," this poem was composed in October, 1938. It was published in the February, 1939, issue of the London *Poetry* and appeared in *The Map of Love*.

SUMMARY

> On the impending birth of Llewelyn (January, 1939), during the period of the impending war, Thomas advises his future son what to expect.

Analysis. A saint is about to emerge from the heaven of the womb and, like Wordsworth's "Intimations Ode," begin a process away from angelic vision and glory. Life on earth is worse than can be imagined - singing, burning, lurching and sinking in rough seas with a cargo of worthless leeches and straw. The final **stanza** exhorts the unborn baby to cast aside fear of birth because he is gentle and will bring joy into the world, compensating for the horrors of the world.

Form And Style. "A Saint About to Fall" is written in three **stanzas** of seventeen lines each, each **stanza** constructed of four quatrains plus one line. The **imagery** and the **syntax** are obscure, but the emotions involved in this poem are such that the reader feels its message by intuition rather than deciphers it. The **rhyme** is an abab type.

IF MY HEAD HURT A HAIR'S FOOT

Introduction. Composed in March, 1939, and first published in the London issue of *Poetry* the following month, this poem is among those in *The Map of Love*.

SUMMARY

The poem is a dialogue between an embryo, who offers to remain where he is if his birth should cause his mother pain, and the mother, who replies that he must be born and that he must follow by necessity the life process.

Analysis. The embryo declares that if his emerging head hurt even a single hair root or his breath pain his mother, she must push him back into the womb or kill him. He would rather strangle in the umbilical cord than hurt love. He would rather do anything than rip his mother open and bloody her. The womb is the creation of destruction and pain, if the embryo should hurt his mother, he should be pushed back into the womb. The mother replies with an emphatic "No!" Caitlin would not exchange the birth to come with Christ's heaven or a soft, pearly sleep. She tells the embryo of the home and voice that await him when he enters the world; he must thrust himself out, regardless of the pain. She further advises him that he has no choice, he must necessarily be born since he has already begun the process of life-death.

Form And Style. The poem is divided into two sets of three five-line stanzas. The sprung rhythm is excellent and freely moving. Every tonal technique, characteristic of Welsh poetry, is here: **alliteration**, assonance, **consonance**, and internal rhyme.

TWENTY-FOUR YEARS

Introduction. "Twenty-Four Years" was composed in October, 1938. It appeared in the December, 1938, issue of *Life & Letters Today* before its publication in *The Map of Love*.

SUMMARY

His twenty-fourth birthday reminds Thomas that life is a process of death.

Analysis. Twenty-four years bring tears to Thomas' eyes when he recalls that he crouched in his mother's womb like a tailor making a shroud for his initiation into life-death. He dressed himself in the shroud of flesh and bones to journey through life to death and decomposition into elements. He will continue down this road for as long as forever lasts.

Form And Style. This poem is comprised of only nine lines. The rhyme is in an abbcddcda pattern, again based on terminal sounds.

QUESTIONS ON THE MAP OF LOVE

Question. What are Thomas' thematic concerns in this volume of his poetry?

Answer. Thomas has expanded his **themes** to include the upcoming marriage to Caitlin Macnammara and the threat of impending war. There are several poems on the writing of poetry, either the poet's intent or the poet's technique. Thomas still refuses to accept death or the dogmatism of the church. The future birth of this son, Llewelyn, presents a new aspect of the birth cycle in Thomas' verse.

Question. Has there been any development in Thomas' style or technique?

Answer. Yes. Thomas is becoming more lucid as he progresses from darkness toward the light. The use of ambiguous symbols is decreasing and the use of **metaphor** is increasing. There is a greater ease in handling his statements and technique, with a lengthening of sentences and grammatical units. His obsessive sexual preoccupations are being replaced with the greater expression of powerful and poignant feelings for others.

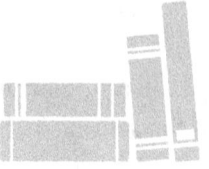

MAJOR POEMS

DEATHS AND ENTRANCES

THE CONVERSATION OF PRAYER

Introduction. This opening poem of *Deaths and Entrances* was composed in March, 1945. Before publication in book form it appeared in the July, 1945, issue of *Life & Letters Today* and the July 16, 1945, issue of *The New Republic*.

SUMMARY

The mechanical, ritualistic prayer of a child is ignored, but the sincere, conversational prayer of the man is rewarded.

Analysis. Prayers are about to be said by the man on the stairway who is going up to his dying wife's room, afraid she is dead, and the child in bed who is not concerned with the object of his prayers but wants to sleep in a safe land. But there is a reversal: the father finds calm and peace in his wife who is alive and warm; the child inherits a nightmare fear of death.

Form And Style. The poem is composed of four five-line stanzas. The **rhyme** scheme is interchanging, that is, not only the terminal sounds rhyme but also at the break (chiasmus) in the middle of the line: b-a, a-b, d-c, c-d, b-a. Terminal **rhyme** is represented by the second letter of each pair.

A REFUSAL TO MOURN THE DEATH, BY FIRE, OF A CHILD IN LONDON

Introduction. "A Refusal to Mourn" was written in March, 1945. It appeared in *The New Republic* on May 14, 1945, and in *Horizon* in October of that same year. It was published in *Deaths and Entrances*.

SUMMARY

As long as he is alive Thomas will refuse to mourn the child's death or allow his art to degenerate into-propaganda. Only silence is appropriate, for after the first death, there is no other death.

Analysis. Not until Thomas himself and the universe enter the final seconds of existence, not until Thomas completes the process of Time and becomes one with nature, will he perform the least act of mourning for the child who died in a bombing raid on London. It would be murder and blasphemy to repeat elegies. Only silence is proper at such a time.

Form And Style. The poem is written in five **stanzas** of six lines each, the second and fifth lines being short. The **rhyme** is abcabc. The first sentence extends to the first line of the third stanza. The final line, terse and powerful in its effect, achieves its impact because it is so short in comparison with the previous sentences and because it is so unexpected.

POEM IN OCTOBER

Introduction. "Poem in October" was composed in August, 1944. It was published in the February, 1945, issue of *Horizon* and in *Deaths and Entrances*.

SUMMARY

The freshness of nature reverses Thomas' morbid concern with birth-death to a wonder at summer and a promise to continue singing life's mystery.

Analysis. On his thirtieth birthday Thomas wakes in the morning to the sound of birds and rolling sailboats in the harbor. It was rainy as he got up, early before the town awoke, and walked down the road out of town. He climbs a hill, listening to the birds in the trees, and looks back at the dwindling town through misting rain. But the weather changes and becomes a bright, blue-clear summery day. Thomas recalls the times he walked with his mother through the sunlight and green orchards. These were the woods where a boy was happy and the mystery of this joy sang in the scene around him. The weather turns again and Thomas prays that his heart's truth may be sung again on the following year.

Form And Style. Written in a freer form and rhythm the words flow beautifully along the lines of differing length. Each

stanza has the same shape, shortening toward the center and end, with a longer final line for visual balance. Aural and visual **imagery** combine to make this an excellent poem. There is no **rhyme**, but the **assonance** of the terminal words presents a progressive unity.

THIS SIDE OF THE TRUTH

Introduction. Dedicated in parentheses to Llewelyn, this poem was composed in March, 1945. It appeared in the July issue of *Life & Letters Today* and *The New Republic* of July 26th. It was published in *Deaths and Entrances*.

SUMMARY

Thomas tells Llewelyn that there is no judgment of the moral value of a person's acts or wishes because heaven is indifferent and death is universal and final.

Analysis. Youth cannot see the truth that, under an unconcerned heaven, innocence and guilt are undone and have as much meaning as dust on the road. Moral right and wrong evaporate and blow away in the dark and death which are neither good or bad. One's thoughts and actions, whether good or bad, have been predestined and will not be judged after death.

Form And Style. The poem is composed of three **stanzas** of short (two or three-stressed) lines. The rhyme-scheme is simple: abcabcdefdef.

TO OTHERS THAN YOU

Introduction. Written in May, 1939, "To Others Than You" was published in the Autumn, 1939, issue of *Seven* and in *Deaths and Entrances*.

SUMMARY

> This poem is a diatribe against "friends" who turn out to be deceiving and betraying enemies.

Analysis. The poem opens with a single-line **stanza**, calling Thomas' friend by the word "enemy." This friend had learned the inmost secret of Thomas and betrayed his trust; he had a hammer-hand under a velvet glove. Although Thomas loved his friends, even for their faults, he realizes now that they are enemies standing on stilts to be able to pry further into his secrets.

Form And Style. The first **stanza** contains only one line and challenges the enemy. The second **stanza** of sixteen lines lists the ways Thomas has been betrayed. The final **stanza**, of four lines, contains the conclusion that his friends were enemies. The **rhyme** is complex and difficult. The lines contain four stresses or, sometimes, three stresses.

LOVE IN THE ASYLUM

Introduction. This poem was composed about 1941. It appeared that Spring in the London issue of *Poetry* and was published in *Deaths and Entrances*.

THE MAJOR POEMS

SUMMARY

> "Love in the Asylum" depicts the return of poetic inspiration in the form of a mad girl sharing Thomas' room and bed in a mad house.

Analysis. A stranger has entered Dylan's room in a mad house to share it with him. The stranger is a girl who is as mad as birds and who enters the poet's bed. She deludes the mad house by bringing with her clods (Wordsworthian?) and deludes the room by walking. She is possessed and Thomas, making love to her, undergoes the same vision of creativity that made the stars.

Form And Style. The poem is written in six **stanzas** composed of three lines each. **Rhyme** and structure divide the poem into two parts. The first part **rhymes** abc abc abc; the first and third lines are short and the second line is long, but in the following two **stanzas** the length is reversed. The second part **rhymes** def def def, and is constructed in the same way as the first part. The first period occurs at the end of the first part, indicating a break in thematic presentation - she is the deluding stranger. In the second part she is possessed by vision and by Thomas.

UNLUCKILY FOR A DEATH

Introduction. Composed in May, 1939, and published in the October issue of *Life & Letters Today*, this poem was revised about January, 1946, and published in *Deaths and Entrances*.

SUMMARY

> Originally titled "Poem (to Caitlin)," "Unluckily For a Death" shows Thomas rejecting the guilt feelings associated with sex and proclaiming it the holy and only way of achieving immortality.

Analysis. The subject and verb of the first sentence are not found until the second and third lines of the second **stanza**. Unluckily for death and the woman, Thomas' body is holy and fortunate when caught and kissed in the woman's body. Since sex is a religious ceremony, and the female sex organs a god, there should be no guilt to loving and copulating by the sea-sperm. Continence is not a virtue, love is sacred and death is defeated by intercourse. Thomas will not chant orthodoxy while he can read the sacred word in the passionate gyrations of his partner's body. Continence is guilt, producer of monsters and sexual abnormalities. Physical love instructs that heavenly resurrection through self-denial shall fail; immortality shall come through sexual love because Paradise is the woman's body.

Form And Style. This poem is composed of four fourteen line **stanzas** of obscure and intricate **syntax**. The **rhyme** is approximate.

THE HUNCHBACK IN THE PARK

Introduction. This poem, one of Thomas' earliest, was composed May 9, 1932. It was revised in March, 1938 and published in *Criterion* in October, 1938. It was published in *The Map of Love* but Thomas placed it among the poems of *Deaths and Entrances* when he was preparing his *Collected Poems* for publication in 1952.

SUMMARY

> The hunchback, a memory from Thomas' childhood days in Cwmdonkin Park, parallels the poet, creative, solitary and cut off from society.

Analysis. The hunchback, sitting in the park from its opening to nighttime, drinking water and eating bread, slept at night in a dog's kennel although he was not chained up. The schoolboys would tease him and mock his deformity, just as people with the mentality of school children mock the poet whom they consider mentally deformed. The old hunchback would doze in this park filled with children, imagining tigers in the jungle and sailors. He would dream of a straight, tall woman, actually creating her in his mind so that she might stand in the night after he had returned to his kennel, followed by the innocent boys.

Form And Style. The seven **stanzas** of this poem contain six lines each. The sprung rhythm moves with varying stresses within the lines. The rhyme scheme is an abbaba pattern.

INTO HER LYING DOWN HEAD

Introduction. This poem was composed in June, 1940, and published that November in *Life & Letters Today*. It was revised about January, 1946, and published in *Deaths and Entrances*.

SUMMARY

> Thomas becomes jealous when he dreams that Caitlin is dreaming of her previous, real or imaginary, sexual partners.

Analysis. Thomas' enemies enter Caitlin's bed through her ear or under her eyelids, rekindling the passions aroused in her by passing strangers, or her adolescent lover who took her virginity in a hayloft, or all of England stroking her loins. In the second part, Caitlin moans in her dream (in Thomas' dream) and his faith in her disintegrates. Jealousy enters Thomas' unhappy bed, and he imagines all the previous sexual experiences Caitlin had before they met. The third part metaphorically presents the husband and wife as two grains of sand, independent beings, yet lying together on the beach. The female declaims infidelity in the dream but is innocent, the male mourns in his self-contained shell. His enemies rest and bury their dead.

Form And Style. The poem is divided into three parts of twenty-three lines each. The rhyme-scheme, if it can be called such, is approximate. The rhythm flows through the varying stresses on lines of differing lengths.

DO NOT GO GENTLE INTO THAT GOOD NIGHT

Introduction. Addressed to his father, "Do Not Go Gentle..." was composed in 1950. It was published in the magazine *Botteghe Oscure* in 1951, in *Partisan Review* in America, and in the last volume of Thomas' verse, "In Country Sleep". Thomas placed it among the poems of *Deaths and Entrances* in 1952 for the publication of his *Collected Poems* by New Directions.

THE MAJOR POEMS

SUMMARY

Thomas advises his father, who has lived "gentle" all his life, to be bold and rebel against a quiet acceptance of death.

Analysis. Do not die gently because old age should rage and fight against death. Although wise men know that nothingness awaits them after death, they do not die gently because they spoke the truth during life. Good men, who lived morally proper lives, fear that their deeds may not be good enough and so do not die gently. Wild men who reached for the heavens and sang of it, do not die gently. Serious, grave men see that blind eyes could be bright and blazing, and they do not die gently. And you, father, curse or bless me but do not die gently. Rage out against death.

Form And Style. "Do Not Go Gentle into that Good Night" is written in the form of a villanelle: five or more tercets and a concluding quatrain, using only two rhymes. The first line must end the second and fourth tercets, the third line must end the third and fifth tercets, and the first and third lines must be the third and fourth lines of the quatrain. The rhyme-scheme is aba aba aba aba aba abaa. The poem is written in iambic pentameter.

DEATHS AND ENTRANCES

Introduction. This poem, which gave its title to Thomas' book of war-time verse, was composed in 1940. It was published in the January, 1941, issue of *Horizon* and in *Deaths and Entrances*.

SUMMARY

> The threat of German invasion, when death will come to close friends and strangers by aerial bombardment, is increasingly close.

Analysis. On an evening of incendiary bombardment there will be several near hits and near deaths and several hits and deaths, among them at least one of the poet's closest friends. On this incendiary evening, a fellow Englishman, a stranger to the poet, will weave in dog fights and die to save the poet. On this incendiary evening an enemy will seek out the poet, and in a roar and flash of thunderbolts blot out the sun.

Form And Style. Each of the three **stanzas** begins with the same line. The twelve lines of each **stanza** contain alternating long and short lines, except the tenth and eleventh lines, which are both short. The **rhyme** is near-rhyme, abcabcdefedf. The title is taken from John Donne's last sermon, "Death's Duel, or, A Consolation to the Soule, Against the Dying Life, and Living Death of the Body:" ..."the death of the wombe, is an entrance, a delivering over to another death, the manifold deathes of this world."

A WINTER'S TALE

Introduction. "A Winter's Tale" was composed in March, 1945, and printed in the July edition of *Poetry*. It was published in *Deaths and Entrances*.

THE MAJOR POEMS

SUMMARY

An old man, alone in a farm house in the winter, prays for love. A she-bird arrives in a vision and brings him love and death.

Analysis. It is a winter's tale that the snowy twilight glides over the countryside and around the farmyard and houses. Once a man alone in the farmhouse opened the scrolls of fire in his head and heart, burned them and prayed at the point of love. He was forsaken and afraid. His naked need struck him, bound him burning and lost seeking the inhuman cradle and the bridal bed. He cried for deliverance. Outside the wind and time sang in the snowfall. Outside there was a she-bird, brilliant like a bride, and the farmyard exulted as though in a ritualistic love dance. The she-bird flew up and the man chased her through the countryside until she descended on a hill near the farm. The tale is ended, the dancing and singing stopped. The bird is bedded and the man, wedded through her thighs, is brought low and burning in the bed of love. Her sex organs are paradise and the she-bird rose with him flowering in her melting snow.

Form And Style. This poem is composed of twenty-six **ballad stanzas** of five lines. The first line of each **stanza** is short. Tonal quality is excellent in this fine-sounding poem, built up by rhythm, **alliteration** and assonance.

ON A WEDDING ANNIVERSARY

Introduction. "On a Wedding Anniversary" was composed about 1939, and it was first published in the March 15, 1941, issue of *Poetry*. It was revised about January, 1946, for publication in *Deaths and Entrances*.

SUMMARY

> The war and the Nazi bombers destroy love and the harmony of marriage.

Analysis. On the third anniversary of a marriage the sky is torn open. Now their love is lost because from every true cloud and bomber-concealing cloud Death falls on the couple's house. Because of their love, a series of events began which terminated in their destruction and separation, but this destruction is also a unification because their elements merge in the Holocaust.

Form And Style. This short poem is written in three quatrains with a **rhyme** scheme of abba/acca/cddc. The first lines of each **stanza** are short. **Alliteration** and **assonance**, coupled with the rhythm of three and four-stressed lines, move the lines briskly along.

THERE WAS A SAVIOUR

Introduction. This poem was composed in February, 1940, and published that May in *Horizon*. It was later printed in *Deaths and Entrances*.

SUMMARY

> In a winter early in the war, Thomas excoriates nominal Christians who did not practice Christian charity and the

> teachings of Christ and who are now left with the result - the destruction of war.

Analysis. There once was a very rare and common saviour whom children who were kept from the light of natural truth and people imprisoned by their wishes studied. His safe unrest was calming and men could hide their fears in Christianity's teachings, remaining silent when madness increased on the earth. The sound of the churches was glorious and those who did not object when men died, put their cheeks against a bursting cloud from an anti-aircraft shell. In the dark there is only yourself now and myself, who did not object to aggression and death but buried ourselves deeper in the prayer books. Now we lament and mourn the destruction of others' homes, others' death, and see the dust of strangers entering our own homes. Spiritual exiles before, we now arouse that love which once opened the rocks covering sepulchres.

Form And Style. The poem is an ironic accusation of those who follow the rituals of Christianity, without making its force vital in their lives. The **irony** is further underlined by Thomas' use of the same meter as the hymn of Milton's "On the Morning of Christ's Nativity." The **rhyme** is near-rhyme, based on **assonance**, in an ababccdd pattern.

ON THE MARRIAGE OF A VIRGIN

Introduction. Written on March 22, 1933, this poem was revised in January, 1941. It was published in October, 1941, in *Life & Letters Today*, and in 1946 in *Deaths and Entrances*.

SUMMARY

> Physical love is holy and innocent because the bride loved life and was natural when she was a virgin, and now her love is sacred because it exalts and unites the flesh and the spirit both.

Analysis. Waking alone in the morning in a plenitude of loves because the virgin loved life and was natural in life, the sun leaps out of her thighs. Now, however, she will no longer sleep alone where all her senses were married to nature, for a man sleeps with her and she learns of further miracles of nature in his love-making.

Form And Style. The near-rhyme is built up of **assonance** in the terminal sounds, forming an ababccd pattern. There are two **stanzas** of seven-lines each, making an approximate **sonnet** of seven and seven instead of eight and six, the first part dealing with her love (virginal) for nature and the second part with her love (married) for the extension of nature.

IN MY CRAFT OR SULLEN ART

Introduction. This short poem was composed in 1945 and appeared in the October, 1945, issue of *Life & Letters Today*. It was published in *Deaths and Entrances*.

SUMMARY

> "In My Craft Or Sullen Art" is a poetic manifesto that Thomas' craft is exercised only for lovers, who, however, pay no heed.

Analysis. In his craft, exercised at night when the moon is out and lovers are in bed, Thomas works, not for glory or profit or reputation, but for the lovers' inmost hearts. He does not write for the proud man, isolated from others, or for the dead (who have their psalms), but for lovers who do not praise his art or buy his volumes or even pay any attention to his poetry.

Form And Style. Written in two **stanzas** of eleven and nine lines, rhyme appears occasionally. Most of the lines contain three stresses. There is some **alliteration**, but the major tonal device is assonance.

CEREMONY AFTER A FIRE RAID

Introduction. "Ceremony After a Fire Raid," another of those few poems which does not take its title from the first line of the poem, was composed in early 1944. It was published in *Our Time* in May, 1944, and in *Deaths and Entrances*.

SUMMARY

The death of a new-born baby during an air raid makes Thomas pray for forgiveness for participating in the cause of the baby's death before it could contribute anything to society.

Analysis. The first part expresses Thomas' grief at the death of a child a few hours old, charred sucking its mother's breast. He expresses the darkness when the incendiary broke into the child; miracles cannot atone for his death. He asks the child to forgive us its death so that its death will grow through our hearts. He tells the child to cry while they chant in the streets dwarfed by the towering flames of burning London. In the second part Thomas sermonizes, identifying the child with Adam and Eve, the Virgin Mary and Christ. The myth of Adam and Eve (the **theme** of life-death brought into the world) is always in Thomas' Sunday service over the dead children dying in the flash and flesh of light. The third part is a triumphant doxology ("Gloria in excelsis") in which the masses of the ocean (a symbol of death) bearing the infant erupt to eternally sing glorias into the organs of the burning cathedrals, burning weathercocks and burning clocks over the funeral pyres of the city. The child has become a eucharist in the flames of London.

Form And Style. The first part is composed of four stanzas, three **stanzas** having eight lines, the third stanza having seven lines. The stanzas begin with lines of two syllables, followed by a second line of three syllables, and a third line (except in the third **stanza**) of one syllable. The **rhyme** is based on terminal letters in the following pattern: abcdedce/abbbcdcd/aabcdcr/ aabcdcec. The second part is one twenty-eight line **stanza** of intricate and convoluted **rhymes** of mixed three and four-stresses. The third part is one **stanza** containing seventeen lines of mixed stresses. The **rhyme** is easily discernible as an aabacbdceeffgfgfg pattern.

WHEN I WOKE

Introduction. "When I Woke" was composed about 1939 and published in the Autumn, 1939, issue of *Seven*. It was revised about January, 1946, for publication in *Deaths and Entrances*.

THE MAJOR POEMS

SUMMARY

> Thomas awakes in a morning of the war to the sound of the noises of destruction.

Analysis. When I woke one morning, there was noise in the town. Birds, clock chimes, the crowds in the (burning?) streets, the noises of the sea dinned, while outside was a man with a scythe cutting the morning off, destroying the last snake left. Thomas makes everybody's morning a world of death and the fall of a sparrow and the disintegration of a mammoth. But this morning he has heard a voice in the air saying that the town is destroyed, time and God are no more, and Thomas then draws the white sheet over the corpse of the British Isles. This last part can also be interpreted to mean that Thomas himself is dead and the sheet he draws is his own winding sheet over himself.

Form And Style. "When I Woke" is composed of two fifteen-line stanzas. **Rhyme** appears occasionally, the main technique being **assonance** in the lines.

AMONG THOSE KILLED IN THE DAWN RAID WAS A MAN AGED A HUNDRED

Introduction. This ironic poem was composed in 1941 and printed in *Life & Letters Today* in August. It was later published in *Deaths and Entrances*.

SUMMARY

> Among those killed in a dawn raid was a man when he stepped out of his house with a petition. Since he was uncommon in life (aged 100), let him remain uncommon in death. It is the story of a man about to die of old age being killed.

Analysis. When the morning was beginning in the war, an old man put on his clothes and, stepping out of his door, died. A bomb landed, exploding house and man. Tell the street that he stopped a bomb and time stopped for him. The conclusion is a plea not to dig for the man's remains to put them on a common cart, the heavenly ambulance in the morning has flown away with him and a hundred storks (symbols of both death and life-bringers) perch on the right hand of the sun.

Form And Style. The "Dawn Raid" is composed of fourteen lines and rhyming abbacdcd/efgegf. It is in anapaests. The **irony** occurs in the juxtaposition of life and death and the use of the **sonnet** form to comment on a dying man's violent death.

LIE STILL, SLEEP BECALMED

Introduction. This poem was composed about 1945 and published in June of that year in *Life & Letters Today*. It was published in *Deaths and Entrances*.

SUMMARY

> This poem possibly refers to the survivors of a sinking ship (torpedoed?) who are watching her go down.

Analysis. Thomas tells the sufferer, with a wound in its throat, to lie still and sleep becalmed. All night long they have heard the sound of escaping steam and the inrushing sea in the wound and the voices of the drowned. They heard the sea sing to open a pathway for the sinking ship. Thomas again exhorts the passengers to lie still, and hide the hole in the hull whose mouth calls to them to follow, under the water, or they may obey and ride with their ship down to the ocean's bottom.

Form And Style. This poem is the closest Thomas comes to the traditional **sonnet** form, being composed of two quatrains and a sestet. The **rhyme** is abab/caca/dbadba. The long lines and the four stresses in each line give the rhythm a somber slowness appropriate to the funeral of a ship.

VISION AND PRAYER

Introduction. This intricate image was composed about August, 1944. It appeared in January, 1945, in *Horizon* and was subsequently published in *Deaths and Entrances*.

SUMMARY

These images are a record of Thomas' movement from lost darkness to found light, told in **imagery** of the miraculous birth of his son and his baptism.

Analysis. In the next room a child is being born, brought from the dark blessings of the womb to mortal life. The birth of this baby is miraculous and Thomas must lie still until the wall is torn (the womb is opened) by his head and he is brought to light. When Thomas is able, he will run into the room crying in the caldron of his kiss. The son is equated with the Son of God and the sun of the heavens, and the baby's love with Christ's love for the sinner. There is the flaming Sacred Heart of the babe where Thomas shall be resurrected in a spiraling ascension of land and sea. Thomas dies, because to look on the face of God is to die. Part II: Thomas prays in the name of all the lost, though he has become separate from that group because of his joy, that his son be able to return to the womb before his lips can speak. In the name of lost who believe in the death of the soul at the death of the body Thomas has prayed, and now he prays in the name of pagan lost that the babe let the dead remain dead, that they avoid the christening consequences of Gethsemane and the Resurrection, because eternal death and blackness is a comforting thought. In the name of the unborn Thomas next prays that death shall remain the end of all things. Thomas has been praying in the name of the lost. But he has been burned in a blessing of the sun and is found, baptised into Christianity. He prays that he himself may be absorbed into the wounds of the Crucifixion. He is now lost in the light of the blinding Son.

Form And Style. The word "form" in this section of commentary is very appropriate to a discussion of "Vision and Prayer." The first part of six sections is in the form or image of a diamond: the first line is monosyllabic and each succeeding line adds one syllable until there are nine syllables, and then the process is reversed. The second part does just the opposite, it is in the shape of a wing or chalice. The lines **rhyme** aabbcc, etc.

BALLAD OF THE LONG-LEGGED BAIT

Introduction. "**Ballad** of the Long-legged Bait" was composed about May, 1941. It was published in *Horizon* in July, 1941, and later in *Deaths and Entrances*.

SUMMARY

The "**Ballad**" presents the **epic** struggle of all men against the assaults of the flesh, and the ultimate vanquishment of sinful concupiscible lusts by sublimation to a higher love. The poem is a miniature religious **ballad** of man's redemption, not by Christ's grace, but by his own power.

Analysis. The fisherman's boat slides through the waters of the bay heading for the sea, its breeze already stirring his hair, leaving behind the shore with its fleet of doves and gulls and cobble-stones in the town resounding under the impact of walking feet. The land begs the fisherman not to look back as Lot's wife had so unfortunately done, or to return. He has become the Wandering Jew. He is a fisherman who uses for bait a girl with hooks through her lips who is thrown into the sea alive. But she is his enemy, his lecherous flesh, and all sin in the figure of a woman. Since the shore had whispered good-bye to the fisherman, he now returns the parting with his own good-bye, good-bye to the smug world of hypocrisy. The fisherman detests a cloistered virtue. The bait is thrown into the sea and is married and violated by every denizen of this watery realm. The sea is a symbol of death in Thomas and birth and gestation are the beginnings of death. The long-legged bait enjoys this orgy, and Jericho falls in the lungs of the participants. Just as Jericho was razed (Josuah 6:24) in order that the Chosen People might enter the Promised Land, so the long-legged bait is violated and conquered in order that the fisherman might enter the Promised Land. The fisherman struggles to retain his grasp on the fishing pole because of the thunderous activity underneath the sea, symbolizing the male organ from which the flames of lust are being exorcised through the sacrifice of the girl. She dies and the inanimate and animate parts of Nature rejoice. The bait takes on the aspect of sacrificial, almost sacramental, bread to be food for the birds. The bait is identified as the tempter of erotic night dreams, by whose loss Satan is made helpless against a refinement of what was once a base love. A storm arises and the fisherman reels in his catch, his hair matted with icy spray and foam. Out of this microcosmic struggle of a single man during the labors of the traditional six days the solution for the macrocosmic salvation is achieved. Death to irrational sensual passion is achieved with the attainment of veteran wisdom, "veteran" because it has been tried and because it is the wisdom of age when lust is not as strong as among younger men. A battle is waged over the body of the long-legged bait and it is being sundered. She is breaking apart as do changing things, indicative of the passing of something changeable to a state of permanence. A new field is sown. A way of life is transformed. The change from the fisherman's previously unpredictable way of life to his new life of steadfastness and constancy is mirrored by a change of **imagery** from the oscillating sea to the stolid land. The sinful cities of the countryside have been destroyed along with the long-legged bait and the fisherman returns as a prodigal son to the home where he is loved in a true fashion. After this "Battle of the Atlantic" all that can be perceived is calm desolation. He anchors in the harbor, the anchor (literally) passing through the water and past any possible floral or coral spires that might be underneath. Metaphorically the anchoring can be interpreted as the penetration through the world of the devil to the protection and embracement of a solace, a "church" in the widest sense of the term. The peregrination is over, the fisherman has attained home and possesses his sublimated heart.

Form And Style. The "**Ballad**" is composed of fifty-four quatrains, rhyming either abab or abba. **Alliteration**, internal **assonance**, and the four-stressed lines unite to carry the rhythm along. The variations in the rhyme-structure and the occasional short lines increase the interest in so long a work.

HOLY SPRING

Introduction. "Holy Spring" was composed in November, 1944, and published in the January, 1945, issue of *Horizon* with "Vision and Prayer." It appeared in *Deaths and Entrances*.

SUMMARY

> An occasional poem of getting up on a spring morning after a night of air raids and love-making in which Thomas reaffirms his belief that sex and natural process will continue, even if it is the last time for him.

Analysis. I climb out of a bed in which we have been making love (when the womb, defeater of death, tried to soothe my intimations of mortality, and war proclaimed ruin and death) to greet that war for which I have no enthusiasm but may have to die for in payment for living. I call for a priest and a mirror to see my sins, but both have died or been destroyed in the night raid, and I am as alone in my poetic creativity as the Creator, organizing a universe from Chaos. I do not praise the spring time that is a bright, burning angelic messenger of funeral pyres and grief, but I bless the fall of sperm and upward thrust of my penis in my hollow husk of a body and the collapsing houses, the Nativity and Resurrection, though it be the last time I shall.

Form And Style. This poem is composed of two twelve-line stanzas, the first beginning with "O" and the second with "No." The **rhyme** is based on **assonance**, in a rhyme-scheme of ababcdcdefef. The lines alternately are short or long, except the third and fourth lines which are both short.

FERN HILL

Introduction. The best-known and most anthologized of Thomas' poems, "Fern Hill" was composed in 1945 and printed that October in *Horizon*. It appeared in *Deaths and Entrances*.

SUMMARY

"Fern Hill" is an exultation of the delights and liberty of childhood seen from the viewpoint of a child, concluding, however, with a sense of mortality and natural process. The poem describes Thomas' youthful years spent on his aunt's and uncle's farm when his aunt, Ann Jones, was still alive.

Analysis. When Thomas was young and carefree on his aunt's farm, Time let him be happy, thinking that he had a long existence to cover into the future. Dylan was lord and ruler in the farmyard and orchards, hunter of the farm animals, innocent victim of Time's mercy. All the days in the entirety were lovely and happy, and nights full of sound. In the morning the farm was like the Garden of Eden and Genesis, before Time began its process. Heedless of Time and ignorant of Time's process of initiation into death, Dylan spent his days happy and carefree and careless, a piper of songs of innocence, unconcerned that Time would soon take him out of innocent grace to the dark shadows of the death process. Time held Dylan young and innocent and, simultaneously, dying.

Form And Style. Composed of six nine-line stanzas, this poem is the most overtly naturalistic of Thomas' poems. The **imagery** of spring and summer, accentuated by the use of the word "green," the easy rhythm of vowel sounds, the variation of stresses in long and short lines, make this an excellent poem. The introduction of time and implications of the life-death form an undercurrent of opposition to the green and golden days of innocent happiness. It is the period of youth trailing clouds of glory before the visionary gleam is lost in Wordsworthian intimations of mortality. "Fern Hill" is a perfect lyric expression of innocent youth in nature.

QUESTIONS ON DEATHS AND ENTRANCES

Question. What are the major **themes** of Thomas' wartime volume?

Answer. Thomas is more and more concerned with death because of the death caused by the war around him and because he had premonitions of an early death. There is a strong movement towards the light of God and the unification or communion of God and man. Thomas is gaining an insight into the sacramental nature of the universe in its relation to God.

Question. Has there been any change in Thomas' style?

Answer. Yes. Because his **themes** were more universally valid (instead of introspectively limited) there is an increased clarity in Thomas' verse of the 1940's. The use of **metaphor** and freeing of rhythm and **rhyme** patterns are further improvements in his style during this period. He was gaining maturity in outlook and in craftsmanship, and this is evident in these poems.

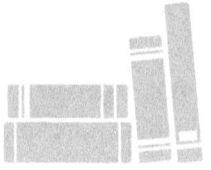

MAJOR POEMS

IN COUNTRY SLEEP

IN COUNTRY SLEEP

Introduction. "In Country Sleep," the last poem of the volume by the same name, was moved by Thomas to the first position when he collected his poems in 1952. This poem was originally intended to be part of a larger, never completed, poem called "In Country Heaven." "In Country Sleep" was composed in 1947 and first published in *Horizon* in December, 1947.

SUMMARY

Thomas prays for his daughter to fear or believe neither childhood's phantasms in the dark woods nor the day of the Lord which comes as a Thief in the night (2 Peter 3:10); Faith in a holy nature will conquer these fears.

Analysis. In the first part Thomas tells his sleeping daughter never to fear the wolf of the fairy tales, no witchcraft shall befall her before the dawn, no country ghost or spell shall transform her. Do not fear future sexual intercourse of the cold prince, bringing destruction. But fear the Thief: the country is holy, it is blessed to be held there, but the Thief will slyly continue to find a way to bring death to her world. The holy music and psalms of Nature give illumination on the Thief who comes in the night. Death will come in the night as part of the process of nature to steal her faith in nature, but he will be unable to so long as nature and life continues each day.

Form And Style. The first part contains nine seven-line stanzas, each fifth line being an indented line of four syllables. The second part contains eight six-line **stanzas** with a short fourth line. The **rhyme** of the first part is abcbaac, of the second part abbcca. There are five or six, sometimes more, stresses in the long lines, and two stresses in the short lines. The **rhyme** is abounding in assonance.

OVER SIR JOHN'S HILL

Introduction. Written in 1948, this poem appeared the following year in *Botteghe Oscure*. It was then published in *In Country Sleep*.

SUMMARY

> Thomas is Nature's priest, reading in her psalter and praising the justice of the natural process of life and death illustrated by the killing hawk and the killed sparrows.

Analysis. Sir John's hill, at Laugharne, is the setting for the drama of life and death. The hawk flying in the burning heights of the sky drops and executes the sparrows in the hedges. Slowly the heron, stalking for fish, lowers his headstone-shaped head. In this crackling war of nature Thomas opens a page of the psalter and reads of death and praise for the hawk and sparrows who participate in the process of creation-destruction, life-death. Thomas and the heron ask God to have mercy on the sparrows because of their songs. Only the stalking heron is left to make the music for the slain birds, and he is likewise a slayer.

Form And Style. The **rhyme** is complexly built upon **assonance** in an aabccbdeaeff pattern. The six **stanzas** contain twelve lines each. There is a flexible pattern of **alliteration**, **assonance**, stresses and emotion-charged onomatopoeia.

POEM ON HIS BIRTHDAY

Introduction. This poem was written about 1950 or 1951. It was first published in World Review in October, 1951. It was included in *In Country Sleep*.

SUMMARY

Thomas moves with more triumphant faith in holy nature and confidently proclaims a hosanna to natural process.

Analysis. In the yellow sun by the river and bay, in his house on the hill, Thomas celebrates his thirty-fifth birthday. Under and around him are the fish and birds working their ways to their deaths, while the poet also works toward the ambush of his wounds. While he writes his poetry toward anguish and grief, birds and fishes continue their natural involvement in the process of life. The boys knell thirty-five bells and Thomas freely goes lost in the light of God. He is joyous in the empty void that is Heaven where he might wander with the ghosts of the dead animals. But dark is a long way off and he must continue in the process of ruin. The closer he moves toward death, the more Nature exults and the more he tackles every wave with increased faith. Nature and the world praise him as he, holy in Nature, sails out to die.

Form And Style. This last of the four poems on his birthday is written in an excellent synthesis of **alliteration**, **assonance** and rhythm. The poem is composed of twelve nine-line stanzas, each odd-numbered line being short. The near-rhyme is schematically ababcdcdc.

LAMENT

Introduction. "Lament" was composed about 1950 and appeared in the 1951 edition of *Botteghe Oscure*. It was revised about 1952 and published in *In Country Sleep*.

SUMMARY

> The poem is an enjoyable, tongue-in-cheek tour de force wherein Thomas sighs that the old ram rod has got caught in marriage, and now the seven deadly virtues plague him.

Analysis. The old rake, dying of women, sighs and recalls his blustery youth when he would sneak into the woods to watch girls playing sports, and run away blushing when they saw him. Or he would make eyes at passing girls. When he was a man and a half he served the town girls and left his prints in their sizzling beds. When he was a real man and the black sheep of the church he was a bull to every woman in the herd; he said that there was time enough before the only reason he would go to bed would be to sleep. When he was half the man he had been, the black sheep of the church was a worn out phallus and he shoved into a woman and found a wife. Now he is no longer a man (the old rake says, dying of strangers), for his wife is religious and bears angels and virtues for him.

Form And Style. The five twelve-line **stanzas** present a progression in age and parallel sexual death (indicated in parentheses). The death is a play on the meaning of ejaculation in intercourse as "death" and the old rake's death at the hands (or thighs) of a virtuous church lady who converts him back to a good life when his sex life is killed. The rhyme-scheme is abcdabcdefef. Anapaests, **alliteration** and onomatopoeia are involved to make this excellent poem a masterpiece of Thomas' recitals.

IN THE WHITE GIANT'S THIGH

Introduction. This poem, part of the projected "In Country Heaven", was composed about 1948 to 1949. It was published in *Botteghe Oscure* in 1950 and in *In Country Sleep*.

SUMMARY

> "In the White Giant's Thigh" is a poem to lusty country girls, barren life, who can produce life when they are dead.

Analysis. The white giant's thigh is supposedly a landmark on a Welsh hill where barren girls would go to gain fertility. Thomas is walking one night on the chalk hill where there is a graveyard of barren women. They may be dead and anonymous, but they still curve and bend in the night's desire as they once made love in the fields or haystacks with country boys. Although their love was unproductive in life, in death they are productive because they teach Thomas that love is always green.

Form And Style. This poem is composed of fifteen quatrains, oddly spaced into **stanzas** of varying length. The rhyme-scheme is abab. **Alliteration** and **assonance** within the lines, combined with the odd spacing and the flexibility of the freely sprung rhythm, contribute to the tonal and rhythmical patterns of the poem.

QUESTIONS ON IN COUNTRY SLEEP

Question. What are the **themes** of the poems in *In Country Sleep*?

Answer. Three of the poems are part of the projected "In Country Heaven." The birthday poem is triumphant acceptance of life and natural process, while "Do not go gentle" is a plea to his father to rebel against acceptance of the natural process. And "Lament" is a comic tour de force satire.

Question. Has there been any progressive movement in his birthday poems?

Answer. Yes. "Twenty-Four Years" (1938) is a morbid statement that life is a journey, or process, to death and decomposition into the elements. "Poem in October" (1944) shows that the freshness of Nature changes Thomas' morbid concern with birth - death to a wonder at summer and a promise to continue singing of life's mystery. "Poem On His Birthday" (ca. 1950) declares a more triumphant faith in holy Nature and contains a confident proclamation of hosannas to natural process.

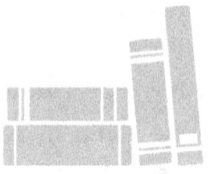

MAJOR POEMS

MISCELLANEOUS

ONCE BELOW A TIME

Introduction. "Once Below a Time" was composed in January, 1940, and appeared in *Life & Letters Today* two months later. It was published only in the 1952 edition of Thomas' *Collected Poems*.

SUMMARY

An autobiographical portrait of the artist as a young dog, in adolescence, disrupting Swansea by his precocious poetry and bohemian manners.

Analysis. Once upon a time, before the present time, when my spirit and body were outgrowing my confining conformings in a Welsh coal-town, I worked in secret with lyric and bold, wolfish rhymes, and burst upon the startled town with bizarre poems and manners and rocketed out of the provincial town to astonish the poetic weavers of London. (Part II:) I hung around the groups of established versifiers in my foolish clothes, not yet really privileged to wear, hoping that I fooled the true poets by my poetic pose. But the master tailors (weavers of **rhyme**) saw through my posturings to the common, ridiculous pretender. It was a relief to behave as a virginal boily boy, instead of conducting a rake's progress, and to lie down and live quietly.

Form And Style. The first part contains two stanzas, written in twelve and sixteen lines respectively. The first **stanza rhymes** abbabcbdede and the second **rhymes** abcabbcdedecedfd. Most of the lines contain three stresses, but some lines are four-stressed. The second part is comprised of four stanzas, all of six lines except the third, which has five lines. The rhyme-scheme is complex, the next-to-last lines of the first and second **stanza** rhyming with the first line of the following stanza. In this part, the stresses are normally four to a line, but there are occasionally five-stresses.

AUTHOR'S PROLOGUE

Introduction. "This day winding down now" was written in 1952 as the prologue to introduce Thomas' arrangement of his *Collected Poems*. The author transports us to his study on the seaside of Laugharne and lets us observe the creative process of writing poetry and understand the meaning of poetry.

SUMMARY

> Because of his love for man and God the poet desires to save all Nature by constructing poetical arks of love against the flood of fear and rage.

Analysis. The first part of this 102-line poem depicts Thomas at his craft - constructing poems - on the seashore of Laugharne. It is the twilight of a late summer's day and Thomas is writing (or singing) his poem to the readers so that they will know how he is concerned thematically with nature and the love of man. The task of writing a poem is compared to the building of an ark which will save mankind from the flood.

The second fifty-one lines continues the building of an ark and explicitly links the poet's function to Noah. The flood is identified with war. Many arks (or poems) will be constructed to save the holy country and spread the doctrine of love. The destructive flood, however, will water the land and make it fertile, ready to receive Thomas' message of love. The flood is therefore both destructive and creative.

Form And Style. Although the "Author's Prologue" appears to be written without **rhyme**, a careful analysis discloses that the lines really rhyme backwards. That is, the first line **rhymes** with the last, the second line with the next-to-last, etc. (abc...xyz/zyx...cba). The auditory pattern is chiefly created by the repetition of internal vowel sounds (**assonance**) and initial consonant sounds (**alliteration**).

The poem opens with a hurrying effect created by using, in the middle of the lines, participles implying motion and process, and by not using punctuation which would slow down the movement of the sentence. The rhythm of the entire poem is sustained by varying the stresses in a line (any number from two to four) and by the technique of **alliteration**. Not only does Thomas' language contribute to the rhythm of the poem but the individual words used also subtly illustrate the auditory and visual images they create. This onomatopoeia perfectly describes the action and also gives the reader the feeling of the action. The sound of the word indicates the action and the selection of that particular word, as well, creates the mood.

The images in the first part deal with the seashore of Laugharne and the fish, shells, and sea-birds. The **imagery** of the second part balances the sea **imagery** with a picture of the woods and its birds and animals. The over-arching **metaphor** of the poet-craftsman, Thomas-Noah, acts as the central idea or image unifying the parts.

Question. What is the importance of the "Author's Prologue"?

Answer. The importance of the "Author's Prologue" is that (1) it introduces the *Collected Poems* in the particular order in which Thomas wanted them presented and (2) it indicates certain **themes** which are found in Thomas' poetry. Because of its conspicuous location this poem presents the reader with certain intimations regarding the body of poetry which follows it. The "Prologue" suggests that Thomas was approaching a religious and sacramental union (or communion) with God and Nature. Thomas still remains at a "poor peace," writing at a feverish pace to overcome the impending threat of a flood of fear and rage. He addresses the birds and animals of nature and a pantheistic God in a time when peace is uncertain and war seems to be near, telling the animals to enter his ark of love in order to be saved. Certain thematic elements - a pantheistic and holy nature, a communion with nature, the concern with the poet's craft, and the function of the poet as vates or prophet - are underlined here. The "Author's Prologue," then, can be considered a preface summarizing Thomas' concerns and themes as they will be developed in the *Collected Poems*.

ELEGY

Introduction. This unfinished **elegy** was arranged by Thomas' friend, Vernon Watkins, according to the various manuscript notes in Thomas' effects. The first seventeen lines are as Thomas wrote them, the remaining twenty-three lines (separated by parentheses) are Vernon Watkin's constructions from the manuscript notes. The poem was begun in 1953.

SUMMARY

"**Elegy**" is addressed to Thomas' agnostic father who had gone gentle into that good night.

Analysis. Although he was too proud to die, he died broken and blinded in the darkest way, brave in his pride. I prayed that he might lie lightly forever, but never lie lost or quietly or find rest but be fathered and found. The veins in his hand were the rivers of the dead and I saw the roots of the sea in his blind eyes. He was a blind, old, tormented man who will never be forgotten by me. He was innocent and died an agnostic, dreading his agnosticism, but stubborn and proud in his agnosticism. Never had he cried in his life, he did not cry at death. I watched life go from his eyes but he sees through his son's eyes. He died, too proud to cry, yet too proud to stop crying, caught between two darknesses. He will not leave my side until I die.

Form And Style. The forty lines of this poem are rhymed in terza rima, aba bcb, etc. Sentences and major punctuation divide some lines into parts, the pauses acting like caesura. It is written in iambic pentameter.

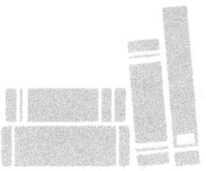

MAJOR POEMS

POEMS

18 POEMS

I See The Boys Of Summer
When Once The Twilight Locks No Longer
A Process In The Weather Of The Heart
Before I Knocked
The Force That Through The Green Fuse Drives The Flower
My Hero Bares His Nerves
Where Once The Waters Of Your Face
If I Were Tickled By The Rub of Love
Our Eunuch Dreams
Especially When The October Wind
When, Like A Running Grave
From Love's First Fever To Her Plague
In The Beginning
Light Breaks Where No Sun Shines
I Fellowed Sleep
I Dreamed My Genesis
My World Is Pyramid
All All And All The World's Lever

BRIGHT NOTES STUDY GUIDE

TWENTY-FIVE POEMS

I, In My Intricate Image
This Bread I Break
Incarnate Devil
To-Day, This Insect
The Seed-At-Zero
Shall Gods Be Said To Thump The Clouds
Here In This Spring
Do You Not Father Me
Out Of The Sighs
Hold Hard, These Ancient Minutes In
The Cuckoo's Mouth
Was There A Time
Now
Why East Wind Chills
A Grief Ago
How Soon The Servant Sun
Ears In The Turrets Hear
Foster The Light
The Hand That Signed The Paper
Should Lanterns Shine
I Have Longed To Move Away
Find Meat On Bones
Grief Thief Of Time
And Death Shall Have No Dominion
Then Was My Neophyte
Altarwise By Owl-Light

THE MAP OF LOVE

Because The Pleasure-Bird Whistles
I Make This In A Warning Absence
When All My Five And Country Senses See

We Lying By Seasand
It Is The Sinner's Dust-Tongued Bell
O Make Me A Mask
The Spire Cranes
After The Funeral (In Memory Of Ann Jones)
Once It Was The Colour Of Saying
Not From This Anger
How Shall My Animal
The Tombstone Told When She Died
On No Work Of Words
A Saint About to Fall
If My Head Hurt A Hair's Foot
Twenty-Four Years

DEATHS AND ENTRANCES

The Conversation Of Prayer
A Refusal To Mourn The Death, By Fire,
Of A Child In London
Poem In October
This Side Of The Truth
To Others Than You
Love In The Asylum
Unluckily For A Death
The Hunchback In The Park
Into Her Lying Down Head
Do Not Go Gentle Into That Good Night
Deaths And Entrances
A Winter's Tale
On A Wedding Anniversary
There Was A Savior
On The Marriage Of A Virgin
In My Craft On Sullen Art
Ceremony After A Fire Raid

When I Woke
Among Those Killed In the Dawn Raid
Was A Man Aged A Hundred
Lie Still, Sleep Becalmed
Vision And Prayer
Ballad Of The Long-Legged Bait
Holy Spring
Fern Hill

IN COUNTRY SLEEP

In Country Sleep
Over Sir John's Hill
Poem On His Birthday
Lament
In The White Giant's Thigh

MISCELLANEOUS

Once Below A Time
Author's Prologue
Elegy

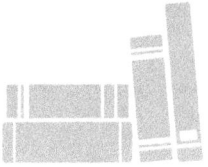

MAJOR POEMS

CRITICAL COMMENTARY

Henry Treece, *Dylan Thomas: 'Dog Among the Fairies'* (London, 1949).

Treece's volume is a collection and expansion of articles he had written for scholarly magazines. He discusses the general characteristics of Thomas, finding that Thomas wrote to expose all his experiences, his style was formal - the use of balanced **alliteration** and half-rhyme, his technical innovations in vocabulary and **imagery** have an emotional affect, and his faults included diffuseness and rhythmic monotony. Treece traces the influence on Thomas of Gerard Manley Hopkins: their identity in outlook, since both tried to illuminate, through individualized vocabulary, some aspect of man; the similarity in their use of compound words; and their similarity in the emotional rush of words brought about by the use of **assonance** and **alliteration**. In addition, Thomas is supposedly indebted to Hart Crane, Swinburne, Rimbaud and Francis Thompson. Treece feels that Thomas' *18 Poems* showed a promise of literary greatness which might have been on a second rank, but this promise was diffused by Thomas' later verse.

Derek Stanford, *Dylan Thomas: A Literary Study* (New York, 1954).

Derek Stanford's book is mainly a commentary on the poems of Thomas, arranged in chronological order by volumes (*18 Poems*, etc.). It is a conducted tour of the individual poems to discover what they are about and what they say about the subjects they deal with. One of the final chapters is an attempt to evaluate Thomas' poetry and analyze his achievements (the extension of literary technique and the revival of a more lyrical way of writing). Stanford feels (and I agree, though perhaps he is too optimistic) that one-third of the *Collected Poems* are good or near-successful. A 1964 paperback reprint includes an added "Literary Post-Mortem" which discusses what recent critics have said about Thomas after his death.

Elder Olson, *The Poetry of Dylan Thomas* (Chicago, 1954).

Elder Olson's book is another excellent commentary on the poems of Dylan Thomas. Dylan Thomas' technique of language is carefully analyzed and discussed. Thomas' powers of symbolism, **imagery** and **metaphor** are explicated. His interpretations and value-judgments are generally outstanding. This book is indispensable to the student of Thomas.

Robert Graves, *The Crowning Privilege: Collected Essays on Poetry* (Garden City, New York, 1956).

Poet Robert Graves' assessment of Thomas is interesting as a view of the Thomas-deprecators. He declares that "Dylan Thomas was drunk with melody, and what the words were he cared not. He was eloquent, and what cause he was pleading, he cared not." He further said that Thomas was deficient in sincerity and conventional and artificial in his poetry.

William York Tindall, *A Reader's Guide to Dylan Thomas* (New York, 1962).

Professor Tindall's volume is an excellent explication of Thomas' poetry, line by line, word by word. Additionally the poems are analyzed stylistically and in their relation to Thomas' life and other work. He contends, "no matter what the ostensible subject of his prose or verse, Thomas always wrote about himself. A poem by Thomas about Jesus, the zodiac, or a worm is about Thomas. What but Joyce did Joyce write about? And yet he wrote about the world, entirely."

Clark Emery, *The World of Dylan Thomas* (Coral Gables Fla., 1962).

Professor Emery's commentary on every poem of Dylan Thomas, with analytic and synthetic explication, must rank among the best of the many works written on Thomas. His volume is a reasoned, comprehensive and definitive study of Thomas' poetry. The poetry is not arranged chronologically by publication in the *Collected Poems*, as is Professor 'Tindall's, but thematically. His book consists of close studies of each poem in an attempt to come to the best possible single meaning, organized thematically into poems revealing the poet as a student of human relationships, as a practicing poet, as a war poet, as a seeker of God, and as an amateur philosopher. The "Introduction" is excellent in assessing the various influences and debts alleged to Thomas.

Ralph N. Maud, *Entrances to Dylan Thomas' Poetry* (Pittsburgh, 1963).

Professor Maud approaches Thomas' poetry without preconceived attitudes, and, by a close reading of certain texts, establishes guiding principles to interpret the poetry. Professor Maud investigates Thomas' recurring themes, his poetic idiom and artistic discipline, using Thomas' own statements, manuscript sources and revisions, textual analysis, biographical and critical material.

Aneirin Talfan Davies, *Dylan: Druid of the Broken Body, an Assessment of Dylan Thomas as a Religious Poet* (London, 1964).

Davies, a close friend of Dylan Thomas, approaches the progression of religious thought and belief in Thomas' verse by demonstration from selected poems. Starting with Thomas' "Note" to the *Collected Poems* and personal knowledge of Thomas (including the little known fact that Thomas attended Catholic services during the war and studied Catholic symbolism and mysticism with a priest in order to widen his poetic range), Davies conceives of the *Collected Poems* as a unified work and shows the remarkable consistency of Thomas' probing into the nature of man and his place in God's creation.

T. H. Jones, *Dylan Thomas* (New York, 1963).

T. H. Jones' book is primarily a biography with commentary on selected poems and prose, concerning itself with the overall view of Thomas the man and the poet. He includes in his analysis Thomas' use of language, imagery and themes. Although Thomas grew up in a period of war, industrial ugliness, mass unemployment and the threat of future war, his poetry has no social reference. His early poems are obsessively about birth, copulation, and sex. There is a lack of progression in Thomas' early volumes and monotony of rhythm, which are offset by linguistic and imagistic activity and by Thomas' robust and all-embracing sense of humor. *The Map of Love* is important because it shows him moving towards both a more direct statement and a concern with life as it actually is, rather than conceived by a highly imaginative adolescent. The importance of his marriage and the war on his poetry is indicated. It was during this period that Thomas is developing towards religious statements; the *Deaths and Entrances* volume makes clear that he is a religious poet. Thomas' later poems show his increasing ability to stand away from and outside his own self and problems and to write objectively. Jones rejects the idea that Thomas' powers were failing in his final poems; rather, these poems are the final flowerings of his genius.

H. H. Kleinman, *The Religious **Sonnets** of Dylan Thomas: a Study in **Imagery** and Meaning* (Berkeley, 1963).

Professor Kleinman's book is a learned and excellent exegesis of Thomas' "Altarwise By

Owl-Light" sonnets, carefully avoiding ascribing to Thomas an erudition which he himself would have denied. Professor Kleinman rejects the theories that Thomas is a surrealist poet, an ultra-Freudian poet, or was a Welsh poet in tradition. He next analyzes Thomas, and concludes that the *In Country Sleep* volume reveals a poet who was certain in his craft, tender in his love, lyrical in his eloquence, and lucid in his meaning. Professor Kleinman reviews the various interpretations of the **sonnets** and states that "I believe that the **sonnets** are a deeply moving statement of religious perplexity concluding in spiritual certainty. They reflect the wonder, awe, doubt, and faith of a young poet who could not reconcile the capacity of a divine pity with the necessity of human sacrifice." Each **sonnet** is a tableau in the tradition of the medieval pageant plays, moving from the Incarnation through the Crucifixion to an apocalyptic prophecy. This is a book which can be enthusiastically recommended and unashamedly praised "to the heavens." Professor Kleinman's book is the best explication of these **sonnets** ever published.

David Holbrook, *Dylan Thomas and Poetic Dissociation* (Carbondale, Illinois, 1964).

Professor Holbrook's book is a minority report against Dylan Thomas. Professor Holbrook finds in Thomas a metaphoric irresponsibility, a lack of maturity, and a tendency toward self-destruction. Using Freudian technique, he finds Thomas' lines disgusting, manifesting sensational morbidity, neurosis, indicating a recoil from life, and meaningless. Thomas, instead of achieving an integration with life, projects a false picture over reality through an impulse to hallucinate.

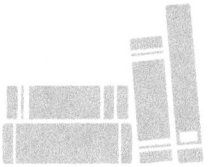

BIBLIOGRAPHY

WORKS BY DYLAN THOMAS

Adventures in the Skin Trade and Other Stories (New York, 1955): this volume contains *Adventures in the Skin Trade* (London, 1955) *and A Prospect of the Sea and Other Stories* (London, 1955)

Collected Poems (London, 1952; New York, 1953)

The Colour of Saying: an Anthology of Verse Spoken by Dylan Thomas, ed. Ralph Maud and Aneirin Talfan Davies (London, 1963)

Dylan Thomas: Letters to Vernon Watkins, ed. Vernon Watkins (London, 1957) Notebooks, ed. Ralph N. Maud (in preparation)

Portrait of the Artist as a Young Dog (New York, 1940)

Quite Early One Morning (London, 1954; New York, 1954): - The British and American editions differ considerably in contents.

"Seven Letters to Oscar Williams (1945-1953)," *New World Writing*, No. 7 (New York, 1955)

Under Milk Wood, a Play for Voices (New York, 1954)

RECORDINGS

Dylan Thomas Reading, Vol. I (Caedmon Records TC 1002): includes "Fern Hill," "A Child's Christmas in Wales," "Do Not Go Gentle into that Good Night," "In the White Giant's Thigh," **Ballad** of the Long-legged Bait," and "Ceremony after a Fire Raid."

Dylan Thomas Reading, Vol. II (Caedmon Records TC 1018): includes "Should Laterns Shine," "Poem on His Birthday," "A Refusal to Mourn the Death, by Fire, of a Child in London," "If I Were Tickled by the Rub of Love," "And Death Shall Have No Dominion," "There Was a Saviour," and "A Winter's Tale."

Dylan Thomas Reading, Vol. III (Caedmon Records TC 1043) includes "A Few Words of a Kind," "Over Sir John's Hill," "The Hunchback in the Park," "On the Barriage of a Virgin," "Light Breaks Where No Sun Shines," "After the Funeral," and "In Country Sleep."

Dylan Thomas Reading, Vol. IV (Caedmon Records TC 1061) includes "A Visit to America" and readings of contemporary British poets.

Under Milk Wood (Caedmon Records TC 2005), Dylan Thomas and the original cast in the premiere performance, 14 May 1953 at the Poetry Center of the New York YM-YWHA.

WORKS ON DYLAN THOMAS

Ackerman, John, *Dylan Thomas, his Life and Work* (New York, 1965).

Annual bibliographies in *PMLA, Philological Quarterly,* and *Year's Work in English Studies.*

Arnheim, Rudolph, et. al., *Poets at Work* (New York, 1948).

Brinnin, John Malcolm, "Bibliography" in *A Casebook on Dylan Thomas* (New York, 1960).

Brinnin, John Malcolm, ed., *A Casebook on Dylan Thomas* (New York, 1957).

Brinnin, John Malcolm, *Dylan Thomas in America* (New York, 1957).

Bullough, Geoffrey, *The Trend of Modern Poetry* (London, 1949).

Cox, Charles B., ed, *Dylan Thomas: a Collection of Critical Essays* (Englewood Cliffs, N.J., in preparation).

Davies, Aneirin Talfan, *Dylan: Druid of the Broken Body, an Assessment of Dylan Thomas as a Religious Poet* (London, 1964).

Day Lewis, Cecil, *The Poetic Image* (London, 1947).

Deutsch, Babette, *Poetry in Our Time* (New York, 1952).

Drew, Elizabeth, and John L. Sweeney, *Directions in Modern Poetry* (New York, 1940).

Durrell, Lawrence, *Key to Modern Poetry* (London, 1952).

Emery, Clark, *The World of Dylan Thomas* (Coral Gables, University of Miami Publications in English and American Literature, VI, 1962).

Frankenberg, Lloyd, *Pleasure Dome: On Reading Modern Poetry* (Boston, 1949).

Fraser, George S., *Dylan Thomas* (London, 1957).

Fraser, George S., *The Modern Writer and His World* (London, 1953).

Fraser, George S., *Vision and Rhetoric* (London, 1959).

Grigson, Geoffrey, *The Harp of Aeolus and Other Essays on Art, Literature and Nature* (London, 1948).

Graves, Robert, *The Crowning Privilege* (London, 1955).

Hendry, J. F., *The New Apocalypse* (London, 1940).

Highet, Gilbert, *Talents and Geniuses: the Pleasures of Appreciation* (New York, 1957).

Hoffman, Frederick, *Freudianism and the Literary Mind* (Baton Rouge, La., 1945).

Holbrook, David, *Llareggub Revisited: Dylan Thomas and the State of Modern Poetry* (Cambridge, Eng., 1962).

Holroyd, Stuart, *Emergence from Chaos* (Boston, 1957).

Hornick, Lita, *The Intricate Image: a Study of Dylan Thomas* (New York, 1958).

Huff, William H., "Works About Thomas," in Elder Olson, *The Poetry of Dylan Thomas* (Chicago, 1954).

Kleinman, Hyman H., *The Religious Sonnets of Dylan Thomas: a Study in Imagery and Meaning* (Berkley, Calif., 1963).

Kunitz, Stanley J., *Twentieth-Century Authors: a Biographical Dictionary of Modern Literature* (New York, 1955).

Maritain, Jacques, *Creative Intuition in Art and Poetry* (New York, 1953).

Maud, Ralph N., *Entrances to Dylan Thomas' Poetry* (Pittsburgh, 1963).

Miles, Josephine, *The Primary Language of Poetry in the 1940's* (Berkley and Los Angeles, 1951).

Miller, James E., Jr., Karl Shapiro and Bernice Slote, *Start with the Sun: Studies in Cosmic Poetry* (Lincoln, Nebr., 1960).

Olson, Elder, *The Poetry of Dylan Thomas* (Chicago, 1954).

Read, Herbert, *The True Voice of Feeling: Studies in English Romantic Poetry* (London, 1953).

Read, William, *The Days of Dylan Thomas: a Pictorial Biography* (New York, 1965).

Rolph, J. Alexander, *Dylan Thomas: a Bibliography* (New York, 1956).

Savage, D. S., *Little Reviews Anthology*, 1947-48 (London, 1948).

Scarfe, Francis, *Auden and After: the Liberation of Poetry, 1930-41* (London, 1942).

Spender, Stephen, *Poetry Since 1939* (New York, 1946).

Stanford, Derek, *Dylan Thomas: a Literary Study* (New York, rev. 1964).

Sweeney, John L., ed, *Selected Writings of Dylan Thomas* (New York, 1946).

Tedlock, E. W., ed., *Dylan Thomas, the Legend and the Poet: a Collection of Biographical and Critical Essays* (London, 1960).

Tindall, William York, *Forces in Modern British Literature: 1885-1956* (New York, 1956).

Tindall, William York, *A Reader's Guide to Dylan Thomas* (New York, 1962).

Treece, Henry, *Dylan Thomas: "Dog Among the Fairies,"* (London, 1949).

Wilder, Amos N., *Modern Poetry and the Christian Tradition* (New York, 1952).

CRITICAL ARTICLES ON DYLAN THOMAS

Adams, Phoebe, "Symbols and Metaphor," *Atlantic*, 191 (May, 1953).

Adams, R. M., "Taste and Bad Taste in **Metaphysical** Poetry; Richard Crashaw and Dylan Thomas," *Hudson Review*, 8 (Spring, 1955).

Aivaz, David, "The Poetry of Dylan Thomas," *Hudson Review*, 3 (Autumn, 1950).

Aiken, Conrad, "The New Euphuism," *New Republic*, 110 (Jan. 3, 1944).

Arlott, John, "Dylan Thomas," *Spectator*, 191 (Nov. 13-27, 1953).

Baro, Gene, "Orator of Llareggub," *Poetry*, 87 (November, 1955).

Beardsley, Monroe C., and Sam Hynes, "Misunderstanding Poetry: Notes on Some Readings of Dylan Thomas," *College English*, 21 (1960), pp. 315-22.

Berryman, John, "The Loud Hill of Wales," in *The Kenyon Critics*, John Crowe Ransom, ed., (Cleveland, 1951).

Bloom, Edward A., "Dylan Thomas' 'Naked Vision,'" *Western Humanities Review*, 14 (1960), pp. 389-400.

Breit, Harvey, "The Haunting Drama of Dylan Thomas," *The New York Times Magazine* (Oct. 6, 1957), pp. 22-26.

Brossard, Chandler, "The Magic of Dylan Thomas," *Commonweal*, 62 (June 10, 1955).

Camborn, Glauco, "Two Crazy Boats: Dylan Thomas and Rimbaud," *English Miscellany*, 7 (1956).

Cane, Melville, "Are Poets Returning to Lyricism?" *Saturday Review*, 37 (Jan. 16, 1954).

Casey, Bill, "Thomas' 'Today, This Insect,'" *Explicator*, 17 (1959), item 43.

Cassill, R. V., "The Trial of Two Poets," *Western Review*, 20 (Spring, 1956).

Chambers, Marlene, "Thomas' 'In the White Giant's Thigh,'" *Explicator*, 19 (1961), item 39.

Ciardi, John, "The Real Thomas," *Saturday Review*, 41 (March 1, 1958).

Ciardi, John, "Six Hours of Dylan Thomas," *Saturday Review*, 41 (Nov. 15, 1958).

Clair, John A., "Thomas' 'A Refusal to Mourn the Death, by Fire, of a Child in London,'" *Explicator*, 17 (1958), item 25.

Condon, Richard A., "Thomas' '**Ballad** of the Long-legged Bait,'" *Explicator*, 16 (1958).

Connolly, Thomas, "Thomas' 'And Death Shall Have No Dominion,'" *Explicator*, 14 (1956).

Cox, Charles B., "Dylan Thomas' 'Fern Hill,'" *Critical Quarterly*, 1 (1959), pp. 134-38.

Daiches, David, "The Poetry of Dylan Thomas," *College English*, 16 (1954).

Emery, Clark, "Two-Gunned Gabriel in London," *The Carrell: Journal of the Friends of the University of Miami Library*, 2 (1961), i, pp. 16-22.

Essig, Erhardt H., "Thomas' '**Sonnet** I,'" *Explicator*, 16 (1958).

Evans, Oliver, "Dylan Thomas' Birthday Poems," *Studies in Honor of Hodges and Thaler* (1962), pp. 131-39.

Evans, Oliver, "The Making of a Poem: Dylan Thomas' 'Do Not Go Gentle into that Good Night,'" *English Miscellany*, 6 (1955).

Evans, Oliver, "The Making of a Poem: Dylan Thomas' 'Lament,'" *English Miscellany*, 7 (1956).

Fitts, Dudley, "The New Poetry," *The Saturday Review of Literature*, 26 (August 28, 1943), pp. 8-9.

Giovaninni, G., "Thomas' 'The Force that through the Green Fuse Drives the Flower,'" *Explicator*, 8 (1950).

Gregory, Horace, "The 'Romantic' Heritage in the Writings of Dylan Thomas," *Poetry*, 69 (March, 1947), pp. 326-36.

Grenander, M. E., "**Sonnet** V from Dylan Thomas' 'Altarwise By Owl-Light' Sequence," *Notes and Queries*, 5 (1958).

Halpern, Max, "Thomas' 'If I Were Tickled by the Rub of Love,'" *Explicator*, 21 (1962), item 25.

Hassan, Ihab H., "Thomas' 'The Tombstone Told When She Died,'" *Explicator*, 15 (1956).

Hawkes, Terence, "Dylan Thomas' Welsh," *College English*, 21 (1960), pp. 345-47.

Hays, H. R., "Surrealist Influence in Contemporary English and American Poetry," *Poetry*, 54 (July, 1939).

Horan, Robert, "In Defense of Dylan Thomas," *The Kenyon Review*, 7 (Spring, 1945), pp. 304-10.

Howard, D. R., "Thomas' 'In My Craft or Sullen Art,'" *Explicator*, 12, (1954).

Huddlestone, Linden, "An Approach to Dylan Thomas," *New Writing*, 35 (1948).

Hynes, Sam, "Dylan Thomas: Everybody's Adonais," *Commonweal*, 59 (March 26, 1954).

Hynes, Sam, "Thomas' 'From Love's First Fever to Her Plague',", *Explicator*, 9 (1950).

John, Augustus, "Dylan Thomas and Company," *Sunday Times* (London), (Sept. 28, 1958).

Johnson, S. F., "Thomas' 'The Force that through the Green Fuse Drives the Flower,'" *Explicator*, 8 (1950).

Johnson, S. F., "Thomas' 'The Hunchback in the Park', and 'The Marriage of a Virgin,'" *Explicator*, 10 (1952).

Jones, Evan, "The Dylan Thomas Country," *Texas Quarterly*, 4 (1961), iv, pp. 34-42.

Jones, Noel A., "Dylan Thomas as a Pattern," *British Annual of Literature*, 6 (1949).

Jones, Robert C., "Thomas' 'The Conversation of Prayer,'" *Explicator*, 17 (1959), item 49.

Joselyn, Sister M., OSB, "'Green and Dying;' the Drama of 'Fern Hill,'" *Renascence*, 16 (1964), pp. 219-21.

Julian, Sister Mary, "Elizabeth Sitwell and Dylan Thomas: Neo-Romantics," *Renascence*, 9 (1957).

Knauber, Charles F., "**Imagery** of Light in Dylan Thomas," *Renascence*, 6 (1954).

Knieger, Bernard, "Dylan Thomas: the Christianity of the 'Altarwise By Owl-Light' Sequence," *College English*, 23 (1962), pp. 623-28.

Knieger, Bernard, "Thomas' 'Light Breaks Where No Light Shines,'" *Explicator*, 15 (1957).

Knieger, Bernard, "Thomas' 'Love in the Asylum,'" *Explicator*, 20 (1961), item 13.

Knieger, Bernard, "Thomas' 'On the Marriage of a Virgin,'" *Explicator*, 19 (1960), item 61.

Knieger, Bernard, "Thomas' '**Sonnet** I,'" *Explicator*, 15 (1956).

Knieger, Bernard, "Thomas' '**Sonnet** II,'" *Explicator*, 18 (1959), item 14.

Knieger, Bernard, "Thomas' '**Sonnet** III,'" *Explicator*, 18 (1960), item 25.

Knieger, Bernard, "Thomas' 'Twenty-Four Years,'" *Explicator*, 20 (1961), item 4.

Korg, J., "**Imagery** and Universe in Dylan Thomas' *18 Poems*," *Accent*, 17 (Winter, 1957).

Lander, Clara, "With Welsh and Reverent Rook: the Biblical Element in Dylan Thomas," *Queens Quarterly*, 65 (1958).

Laurentia, Sister M., "Thomas' 'Fern Hill,'" *Explicator*, 14 (1955).

Logan, John, "Dylan Thomas and the Ark of Art," *Renascence*, 12 (1960), pp. 59-66.

Lougee, David, "Worlds of Dylan Thomas," *Poetry*, 87 (November, 1955).

Mackworth, Cecily, "Dylan Thomas et la double vision," *Critique*, 19 (1963), pp. 500-16.

Maud, Ralph N., "Dylan Thomas' *Collected Poems*: Chronology of Composition," *PMLA*, 76 (June, 1961), pp. 292-97.

Maud, Ralph N., "Dylan Thomas' First Published Poem," *MLN*, 74 (February, 1959), pp. 117-18.

Maud, Ralph N., "Obsolete and Dialect Words as Serious Puns in Dylan Thomas," *English Studies*, 41 (1960), pp. 28-30.

Maud, Ralph N., "Thomas' **Sonnet** I,'" *Explicator*, 14 (1955).

Meyerhoff, H., "Violence of Dylan Thomas," *New Republic*, 133 (July 11, 1955).

Miller, J. E., Jr., "Four Cosmic Poet," *University of Kansas City Review*, 23 (June, 1957).

Mills, Clark, "Aspects of Surrealism," *Voices*, 101 (Spring, 1940).

Mills, Ralph J., Jr., "Dylan Thomas: the Endless Monologue," *Accent*, 20 (1960), pp. 114-36.

Montague, Gene, "Thomas' 'Today This Insect,'" *Explicator*, 19 (1960), item 15.

Moore, Geoffrey, "Dylan Thomas: Significance of his Genius," *The Kenyon Review*, 17 (Spring, 1955).

Moore, Nicholas, "The Poetry of Dylan Thomas," *Poetry Quarterly*, 10 (Winter, 1948).

Morton, Richard, "Notes on the **Imagery** of Dylan Thomas," *English Studies*, 43 (1962), pp. 155-64.

Moynihan, William T., "Dylan Thomas and the 'Biblical Rhythm,'" *PMLA*, 79 (1964), pp. 631-47.

Moynihan, William T., "Dylan Thomas' 'Hewn Voice,'" *Texas Studies in Literature and Language*, 1 (1959), pp. 313-26.

Moynihan, William T., "Thomas' 'In the White Giant's Thigh,'" *Explicator*, 17 (1959), item 59.

Muir, Edwin, "The Art of Dylan Thomas," *Harper's Bazaar*, 88 (February, 1954).

Neuville, H. Richmond, Jr., "Thomas' **'Ballad** of the Long-legged Bait,'" *Explicator*, 23 (1965), item 43.

Nist, John, "Dylan Thomas: Perfection of the Work," *Arizona Quarterly*, 17 (1961), pp. 101-06.

Ormerod, David, "Thomas' 'Twenty-Four Years,'" *Explicator*, 22 (1964), item 76.

Perrine, Laurence, "Thomas' 'Especially When the October Wind,'" *Explicator*, 21 (1962), item 1.

Perrine, Laurence, "Thomas' 'The Hunchback in the Park,'" *Explicator*, 20 (1962), item 45.

Peters, Robert L., "The Uneasy Faith of Dylan Thomas: a Study of the Last Poems," *Fresco*, 9 (University of Detroit, 1958).

Phelps, R., "In Country Dylan," *Sewanee Review*, 63 (Autumn, 1955).

Phillips, Robert S., "Death and Resurrection: Tradition in Thomas' 'After the Funeral,'" *McNeese Review*, 15 (1964), pp. 3-10.

Richmond, Lee J., "Thomas' '**Ballad** of the Long-legged Bait,'" *Explicator*, 23 (1965), item 43.

Rickey, Mary Ellen, "Thomas' 'The Conversation of Prayer,'" *Explicator*, 16 (1957).

Rosenfeld, Paul, "Decadence and Dylan Thomas," *Nation*, 150 (Feb. 23, 1940).

Rhys, Kedrych, "Contemporary Welsh Literature," *British Annual of Literature* (London, 1946).

Scott, Winfield T., "Lyric Marvel," *Saturday Review*, 38 (Jan. 8, 1955).

Sergeant, Howard, "The Religious Development of Dylan Thomas," *Review of English Literature*, 3 (Leeds, 1962), ii, 56-67.

Shapiro, Karl, "Dylan Thomas," *Poetry*, 87 (November, 1955).

Smith, A. J., "Ambiguity as Poetic Shift," *Critical Quarterly*, 4 (1962), pp. 68-74.

Smith, A. J., "The Art of the Intricate Image," *Letterature Moderne*, 7 (1958), pp. 697-703.

Smith, William J., "Life, Literature and Dylan," *Yale Literary Magazine*, 122 (1954).

Spacks, Patricia M., "Thomas' 'In My Craft or Sullen Art' 6-9," *Explicator*, 18 (1959), item 21.

Stanford, Derek, "Dylan Thomas - a Literary Post-Mortem," *Queens Quarterly*, 71 (1964), pp. 405-18.

Stearns, Marshall W., "Explication of Thomas' Poem: 'After the Funeral,'" *Explicator*, 3 (1945).

Stearns, Marshall W., "Unsex the Skeleton: Notes on the Poetry of Dylan Thomas," *Sewanee Review*, 52 (July, 1944).

Stephens, Peter J., "Dylan Thomas: Giant Among Moderns," *Letterature Moderne*, 7 (1958), pp. 697-703.

Sweeney, John L., "Imitations of Mortality," *New Republic*, 126 (March 17, 1952), pp. 18-23.

Symons, Julian, "Obscurity and Dylan Thomas," *The Kenyon Review*, 2 (Winter, 1940), pp. 61-71.

Thomas, R. George, "Bard on a Raised Hearth: Dylan Thomas and his Craft," *The Anglo-Welsh Review*, 12 (1962), xxx, pp. 11-20.

Tindall, William York, "The Poetry of Dylan Thomas," *American Scholar*, 17 (Autumn, 1948), pp. 431-39.

Treece, Henry, "Chalk Sketch for a Genius," *Dock Leaves*, 5 (Spring, 1954).

Treece Henry, "Corkscrew or Footrule," *Poetry* (London) (May-June, 1941).

Treece, Henry, "Dylan Thomas and the Surrealists," *Seven* (Winter, 1938).

Tritschler, Donald, "The Metamorphic Stop of Time in 'A Winter's Tale,'" *PMLA*, 78 (1963), pp. 422-30.

Varney, H. L., and N. N. Kann, "Glamorizing Dylan Thomas," *American Mercury*, 86 (January, 1958).

Wanning, Andrew, "Criticism and Principles: Poetry of the Quarter," *Southern Review*, 6 (Spring, 1941).

Werry, Richard R., "The Poetry of Dylan Thomas," *College English*, 11 (February, 1950).

White, Williams, "The Poet as Critic: Unpublished Letters of Dylan Thomas," *Orient/West*, 7 (1962), ix, pp. 63-73.

Wilde, Martha H., "Dylan Thomas: the Elemental Poet," *Transactions of the Wisconsin Academy*, 44 (1956).

Williams, William Carlos, "Dylan Thomas," *Yale Literary Magazine*, 122 (1954).

Woodcock, George, "Dylan Thomas and the Welsh Environment," *Arizona Quarterly*, 10 (1954).

Ziggerell, James, "Thomas' 'When All My Five and Country Senses See,'" *Explicator*, 19 (1960), item 11.

www.ingramcontent.com/pod-product-compliance
Lightning Source LLC
LaVergne TN
LVHW011717060526
838200LV00051B/2926